EARTH
MEDICINE

EARTH MEDICINE

ANCESTORS' WAYS OF HARMONY FOR MANY MOONS

JAMIE SAMS

HarperSanFrancisco

A Division of HarperCollins*Publishers*

EARTH MEDICINE

Ancestors' Ways of Harmony for Many Moons

Copyright © 1994 by Jamie Sams. All rights reserved. Printed in the United States of America. No part of this book may be used or reproduced in any manner whatsoever without written permission except in the case of brief quotations embodied in critical articles and reviews. For information address HarperCollins Publishers, 10 East 53rd Street, New York, NY 10022.

Book design and illustration by Lory Poulson

FIRST EDITION

Library of Congress Cataloging-in-Publication Data

Sams, Jamie, 1951–

    Earth medicine : ancestors' ways of harmony for many
moons / Jamie Sams. — 1st ed.

        p.   cm.

    ISBN 0–06–-251063–0 (pbk. : alk. paper)

    1. Devotional calendars.   2. Indians of North America—
Religion and mythology. I. Title.

BL560.S27   1994

299'.7—dc20   94–1901

                                            CIP

94 95 96 97 98 ❖ HAD 10 9 8 7 6 5 4 3 2 1

This edition is printed on acid-free paper that meets the American National Standards Institute Z39.48 Standard.

This book is dedicated to the six couples who have shown me that love can be lasting and can endure through all the trials, the years, changes, and tears. I am grateful for their lessons in devotion, their willingness to share their individual creativity, their constant support of one another, their families, and of me. Each couple has made a commitment to share the beauty of their talents with the Children of Earth, to serve in the ways they know how, and to honor the visions they carry in their hearts. Together and individually, we carry the vision of world peace. We use the music we sing, the words we write, the art we create, and the stories we share to create bridges of understanding between all races, creeds, and cultures.

To my friends, the visionaries, who have lived their love and commitment to their mates, believing that a true and lasting love is a rare treasure worth nurturing until the end of time, I am deeply grateful.

Nadia and John York
Patti and Gino Vannelli
Sharon and Joe Ely
Sherry and Ken Carey
Eliza Gilkyson and Reavis Moore
River and Diamond Jameson

You are the Medicine of Earth,
and that Medicine is love.

ACKNOWLEDGMENTS

I would like to acknowledge my parents, Sally and Ross, for their unwavering support, their insight and ability to listen to my heart, and their love of good storytelling, which they have passed to me. You are the loving, uplifting wind beneath my wings.

I gratefully acknowledge my editor, Barbara Moulton, who has maintained her integrity with me at all times, against all opposition. It is a rare individual who is willing to be completely honest and compassionately human in a corporate environment. Her intelligence, sensitivity, and expertise are gifts to our world.

Love to my Dreamwalker, who finally found me, refusing to let me go. You have proved that having faith and trust in the vision of love sent by the Ancestors makes that dream come true. My love, warrior of my dreams—thank you for being.

NOTE TO READERS

For those of you who are reading this book and find it confusing that so many names are capitalized, I would like to give a further explanation. In the Seneca language and in most Native American languages in the original form, certain words are holy or sacred to Native American People. These words are always capitalized in our written languages.

Until recently, few Indian writers were published, and those who were did not have a say as to how the manuscript was dealt with. Harper Collins has shown respect for my work by printing it in our preferred form. For this kind of consideration, I am deeply grateful.

In Native American culture, we see everything as being alive. Each living thing has a specific role as a teacher and family member. Everything on Earth, whether stone, tree, creature, cloud, sun, moon, or human being, is one of our relatives. We capitalize the names of each part of our Planetary Family because they represent the sacred living extensions of the Great Mystery who were placed here to help humankind evolve spiritually. We capitalize Traditions and Teachings because these words represent the equivalent of another faith's holy books.

In Tribal Traditions, we do not consider Grandfather Sun a deity. We do not worship trees or rocks. We do, however, see the Eternal Flame of Love that the Great Mystery placed in all Creation and we honor that spiritual essence. In the Seneca language, we call it *Orenda*. This is the spiritual essence or creative principle called the Eternal Flame of Love that is found inside of all life forms. There is only one Original Source and we call that Creative Source the Great Mystery.

The Thunder Chief, *Hinoh* (Hĕnō), is capitalized because of his role in bringing life-giving waters, without which we could not survive. Grandfather Sun and Grandmother Moon are capitalized because we see them as living beings. The Great Mystery gave them their missions of dividing day from night, bringing light and warmth to our world, as well as pulling the tides of our oceans. In all cases, the words that are capitalized are given respect because of the sacred missions they carry and the extension of the Great Mystery's love that they represent. We teach that all life matters and we honor the Medicines of all life forms as sacred extensions of the Great Mystery's loving plan.

INTRODUCTION

The first calendar that North American Indians ever had was Turtle's shell. Our Ancestors watched the passing of the cycles and seasons, noting that thirteen moons passed before the same seasons returned. Grandmother Nisa (Moon) was our guide. Through her changing cycles, she told women when their bodies were fertile and when they would experience their Moontimes, or menstrual flows. Grandmother Moon disappeared and returned, showing her full face thirteen times during the year. The Earth Mother, who was represented by the most fertile creature on our planet, the Turtle, showed our Ancestors how to mark the passing of each moon cycle. Turtle's shell bore the thirteen moons of the year inside of a frame that formed the circle we call the Sacred Hoop, or Medicine Wheel.

This unifying circle represents the sacred relationship of all life to all life. The Sacred Hoop also represented the path across the sky or orbit that was our Earth Mother's yearly journey around Grandfather Sun. The orbit of Grandmother Moon's journey around our Earth Mother is another circle, giving the Ancestors an understanding of the import of all concentric circles bringing life into unity or harmony.

These thirteen moon cycles gave birth to the legends of the Thirteen Original Clan Mothers who represent the gifts and abilities humankind can develop during the Earthwalk, or physical life. These lessons of developing human potential contain the skills that every Two-legged human must learn in order to live in harmony with all life forms. When we learn what our potentials are and develop the skills of right relationship, we can offer to share those gifts with the whole of the Human Tribe. Generosity is the key to working for the benefit of all living things. If we give of ourselves and of our gifts, the blessings we have received are shared. We can then expand the boundaries and capabilities of all human potential.

When my editor approached me about writing this book, I began to see the value of putting together some lessons or thoughts for each day that could educate the reader about the ways of harmony that have imbued the best of Native American lifestyles. When these concepts are honored, the ideas of living in harmony within a community are easily attainable. Many non-Native friends have asked me to include some of the unspoken rules of etiquette that our Native American community observes in order to bridge potential cultural misunderstandings. I have done this in this text because it benefits our urban Native youths who have not been exposed to the Ancestors' ways as well as educating non-Natives. These lessons of respecting others and their Sacred Spaces can be applied to any culture, resulting in harmonious living.

I was recently surprised when one of my Mohawk sisters told me that she did not know that I had written the poems that begin every chapter in every book that I have authored or coauthored. The only exceptions carry the two names of the writers I quoted. I chose to write some of the thoughts for the day in this text with poetry because the rhythms and cadence of poetry often open our minds to different ways of understanding. Other thoughts for the day are written as Medicine Stories, and all are original. That is to say that these writings are based upon the lessons I have been taught on my path, but none of this text is taken verbatim from other sources.

Harper San Francisco wanted all original material for this book, so I decided to look at events in my life that had taught me about harmony, self-discovery, sharing, love, and more. I then asked for the Great Mystery's guidance. I called on the Clan Mothers' spirits to assist me in knowing which lessons would best represent their creed of Life, Unity, and Equality for Eternity. Then I used my gifts of storytelling and writing to express the beauty of the Ancestors' ways of harmony, creating new material that could reflect these lessons to others. I trust that these lessons, stories, and poems will assist all readers in continuing on their paths of personal healing. My personal desire, in writing this book, is that each one of you claim your right to *become your vision!*

FINDING THE
MEDITATION
FOR THE DAY
⚇

The thoughts for each individual day in this book are based upon the twenty-eight-day moontime cycle of women's menses, *not* the actual orbits of the moon. Since the twenty-eight thoughts per moon are multiplied by the thirteen moons a year, we end up with 364 separate meditations. I understand that this is a very different concept, but it is the human fertility cycle for men and women. Men do not have a different rhythm of creation. All human beings have a female and a male side, bound by the same ebbs and flows of Earth and moon energies.

In ancient times, the orbit of our Earth Mother was different than it is now. Before gold was pillaged from the Earth Mother's body, the waxing and waning cycles of Grandmother Moon took twenty-eight days. The dark or new moon was not counted. We are now experiencing an earth wobble in our orbit that was created by the removal of gold, which was the Earth Mother's tracking system. Consequently, the waxing and waning cycle of Grandmother Moon is now twenty-nine to thirty days and varies from year to year as the axis of our planet shifts.

In order to honor the ancient teachings of the Clan Mothers, I chose to make the use of this book as simple as possible. No matter when a person begins this book, finding where to start reading the thought for the day will be easy. The only thing the reader needs is a regular calendar that has the dates of the new moon and full moon written on each month. It makes no difference what month or day you start reading the book. The daily thoughts will continue until you reach the same moon and day next year.

For instance, if you happened to start this book in April, you would get a regular calendar and find the date of today. Looking at a calendar, make note of the last date prior to today that says new moon. You may have to return to the preceding month. This date is the beginning of April's moon or the fourth moon cycle of the year. The date of that new moon will correspond to the thought for the day numbered 4-1. Now you count the days from that date until today's date.

Let's say that today is April 11 and new moon fell on March 24. March has thirty-one days. By counting the days, with new moon as day one, you arrive at the number 19, and you begin reading the daily thought numbered 4-19. You are now on track and can follow each daily meditation throughout the year. If you lose your place, it is easy to begin again by following the same formula.

For those who do not want to follow the day-by-day plan, this book can also be used as a guidance system. When you are feeling out of balance or overwhelmed, you may sit quietly and keep the book closed in your hands with the binding resting on your lap. Take a few deep breaths to relax your body and still your mind. Reverently ask for the teaching, story, or poem that will nurture you or bring peace to your situation. Take a moment to allow your fingers to feel for the right place among the pages, and then open the book to that page.

This process of asking for answers may be new to some readers. Oftentimes when we are upset, we cannot think clearly, and sometimes we may think that the page we have chosen does not apply to our situation. If we are not calm when we feel which page to open the book to, we may sabotage ourselves. Sometimes the assistance found on the page we are reading is lost on us because we have not relaxed enough to get the lesson. In all cases, we are free to choose another page. The answer we seek will always come to us, if we relax, approaching the situation with a sense of reverence and compassion toward ourselves.

Whether you choose to read the daily thoughts several at a time, only when you feel you need guidance, or following the fertility cycles of the moon makes no difference to me. There are no rigid rules surrounding how these writings are to be used. Readers' enjoyment and singular intuitive growth are more important to me than having them stuck, feeling frustrated because they lost their place in the book.

Some people like structure and others enjoy innovation; that is the beauty of our human uniqueness. I feel that giving examples of several ways that something can be used successfully allows all people their individuality and freewill. Be my guests! Find how these thoughts for the day give you the greatest pleasure and I will have served in the best way I know how. I wrote every day's lesson from my heart, not my head. Asking readers to do anything solely from their heads would be a big mistake. It should be fun—if it isn't, why bother?

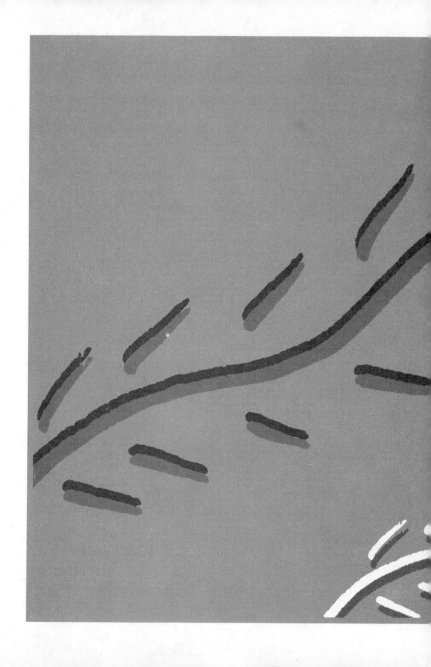

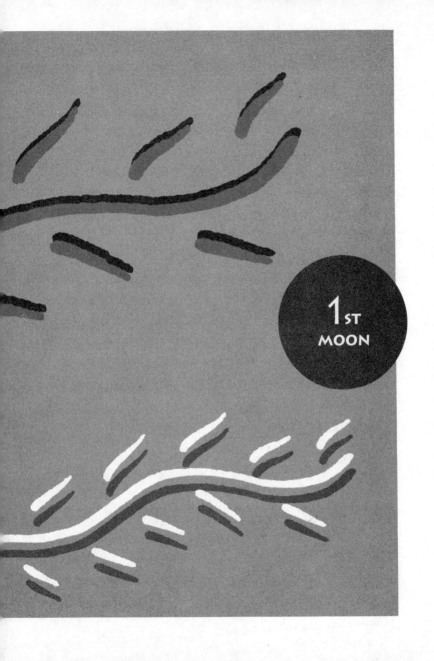

1ST
MOON

RELATIONSHIP TO EARTH AND SKY

The Ancestors teach us that when we wear our hair in braids we honor our connections to the Earth Mother and All Our Relations. Our braids represent our ties to the Earth and the tangible world. When we wear our hair free, we connect our Spiritual Essences to the Spirits that ride on the wind. Our connections to all living things are strong when we honor the truth in each part of Creation and respect the right of all life forms to create life abundant.

Talks with Relations, the Clan Mother of the First Moon Cycle, teaches us to make relatives of our Cousins, the stones and plants; our Brothers and Sisters, the creatures; and our human counterparts of all races and creeds. By honoring these ties to our Planetary Family, we allow ourselves the freedom to be the connecting link between the tangible and intangible, accessing spiritual understanding and the earth-based joy of physicality.

THE FIRST CIRCLE
✖

Our families are the beginning, the first Circle in our lives. This Circle is to be defended with our love, our honor, our integrity, our devotion, our time, our resources, and our words.

The outside world sees us as a product of these commitments. To behave in an unbecoming manner reflects upon every member of the first Circle. If we claim to be spiritual, we must heal the first Circle by being committed to the well-being of every family member without judgment or conditions. Then we *earn* the right to extend the first Circle of blood relations to others whom we adopt through our commitment and love. Only then can we call others "Sister" or "Brother," living this commitment through our willingness to stand in unity through all the tests of time.

Has your need to be right or your refusal to forgive broken your family circle? Has your anger made you belittle other members of your family? Do you have the courage to make amends to those you may have harmed? Can you honor all members for who they are without trying to change their way of being? Can you commit to helping the children and Elders who need your strength and support?

THE CIRCLE OF LIFE
❌

The Circle of Life, the Great Medicine Wheel, has no beginning and no end. Every part of Creation exists as a part of this Circle, and each has a purpose. The Native American way of being speaks of a creed that insists on Life, Unity, Equality for Eternity. Every person who sits in the Circle has a voice, needed talents, and the right to make the world a better place for all living things. The Earthwalk, or life, of each human being will reflect that person's commitment to the whole of Creation. Words are empty commitments unless they ring with truth that is backed with positive actions.

The Clan Mother of the First Moon Cycle, Talks with Relations, teaches us to understand the languages of every part of Creation and to use what we learn to help support all living things. Talks with Relations shows us how to see the overview of how all life forms are interrelated. Each part of the Planetary Family supports the others. To find your place in the Circle of Life, you must ask yourself how you can best assist the Planetary Family by honoring the truth in yourself and then using that truth to assist the whole of the Great Mystery's Creation.

MAKING FAMILY
✄

Earth Mother teach me of my kin,
Of Hawk, and Dove, and flower,
Of blinding sunlight, shady knoll,
Desert wind and morning showers.
Teach me every language of
The creatures that sing to me,
That I may count the cadence of
Infinite lessons in harmony.
Teach me how to honor
The Sacred Spaces of all,
Gently melding with the whole,
Answering the whippoorwill's call.
Steamy tropics to glacial ice,
To thundering ocean tides,
In every grain of desert sands,
Your beauty forever abides.
Oh, Mother of every kingdom,
Let me claim my family's love,
From the whales of deepest oceans,
To the Winged-ones, high above.
Expand my limited vision
Until I can truly know
The missions of my Relations
And the blessings they bestow.

A MATTER OF OPINION

Grandmother Cradle Song was walking through the woods with her granddaughter. When they came to a sun-filled clearing in a stand of alder trees, they decided to rest, allowing the little one to play.

Buffalo Robe occupied herself at the roots of an alder. She was digging a hole while Grandmother sat with her eyes closed, taking in the warmth of the sun. When Grandmother finally noticed what Buffalo Robe was doing, the hole was very large. A pile of earth sat off to the side with the digging stick the girl had been using. Buffalo Robe was nestled inside the hole.

Grandma Cradle Song asked the child what she was doing. The little girl said she had made the hole to allow her to smell the Earth Mother's breath. Grandmother then told Buffalo Robe that she would have to find a new home for the earth that she removed. Buffalo Robe had not thought about that. The little one said she did not think that the soil minded being moved. Grandmother sighed, and then explained.

"Every living thing has a Sacred Point of View, a place where it observes the world. Buffalo Robe, you moved that earth out of its home without permission. You may feel that the soil does not mind, but it is a matter of opinion; every living thing has a right to its Sacred Point of View."

FEAR
✖

The Creature-teachers show us that survival instinct is necessary in the natural world. Being watchful of changes in the weather, of natural predators, and of fire is wise. Being respectful of the hot deserts, the cold glaciers and mountains, and the Sacred Space of other living things shows a deep understanding of survival instinct.

But when a human being succumbs to the irrational fears created in the human mind, that person feeds his or her ignorance of true connection to the Oneness found in the Great Mystery's healing and love.

Talks with Relations, the clan Mother of the First Moon Cycle, teaches us how to honor healthy fear that is born of survival instinct and comes from our animal natures. The language of the Creature-beings is simple to understand if we observe their actions in stillness and silence.

The mental human fear is a different fear. It is like a disease because it is passed through words and future imaginings that have no factual basis in the Now.

MAKING OF RELATIVES SONG
><

You are my Brother; I call you friend.
A fellow warrior, until the end.
And she's my sister, heart to heart.
We've walked the Red Road,
From the very start.

So sing to me of the Beauty Way,
The Ancestors we'll see one day,
Hi yai yai yai yea,
Hi yai yai yai yea.
Yes, sing to me of the Beauty Way,
The Ancestors we'll see one day,
Hi yai yai yai yea,
Hi yai yai yai yea.

When we adopt others into our lives by making them a blood brother or blood sister, we use a Making of Relatives Ceremony. This ceremony is not to be taken lightly, as both parties are committed to the well-being of the other until death. The only way to break this adopted blood tie is if one or both parties betray or break the sacred oath of kinship. In that instance, either person can withdraw the allegiance he or she granted by tearing a blanket in two and burying the pieces in two distant places. This separation is rare because Native People are not casual in their alliances. Once a trust is earned and a vow is given, it is lasting and durable because it is based on the bonds of personal honor and integrity.

LESSONS OF THE FLOWERING PLANTS
✂

Every kind of flower carries a different shape and a different color. Every flower knows it is unique as well as beautiful. The lesson that the flowers show their human Sisters and Brothers is one of love without comparison.

The flowers teach us that every color and shape is individual and beautiful. Without fear or shame, the flowers turn their tiny faces up to catch the love and light of Grandfather Sun. They teach their human counterparts to love the differences in shape and form without comparing the beauty of one over the other. The Earth Mother nurtures every plant, for they are all her children. The Thunder-beings send life-giving rains to water their growth, and all are fed by the light of Grandfather Sun.

It is only human beings who fear that they are less than perfect. They base their unloving judgments upon the authority of other people who are confused, having forgotten that uniqueness and beauty are found in *all* parts of Creation.

LONELINESS
✂

Loneliness only stays to haunt those who have forgotten the presence of their Relations: their Brother and Sisters, the creatures; their Cousins, the plants and stones; their Father, the Sky; and their Mother, the Earth.

We are reminded that our family of Relations is always waiting for us to come and share the beauty of the natural world. When we rediscover their company, we are never alone.

THE CLAN CHIEF OF AIR
✄

Oh, Clan Chief ruling the currents,
Of breeze, and wind, and air,
Fly me through the updrafts,
To soar, where my spirit dares.
Show me the Ancient Spirits
That ride upon the breeze;
Let me learn their wisdom,
To set my heart at ease.
You, who cast the clouds about,
Who bring the tropical storms,
Gusting winds to send me home,
Where I'll be safe and warm,
How is it that you are invisible?
And how do you speak to me?
Is it through feeling your caress,
Or is it the whispers . . .
        you blow through the trees?

Have you ever considered the sacredness of your breath? Without it, we die. It is the only thing that humans cannot live without for more than a few minutes. Is it time to count the breath of life as a blessing?

THE CLAN CHIEF OF EARTH
✖

Sacred Guardian of the Earth,
Of sandy loam and clay,
Keeper of seeds and trees,
And of the flowers' display,
You, who guard the Sacred Stones,
And the legends that they keep,
Watching over the Creatures and
The Mountains while they sleep,
Sing to me your secrets,
Of canyons, hills, and plains,
That I may know the mysteries,
Of why the land remains . . .
A constant source of beauty,
That feeds every Child of Earth,
Nurturing all weary travelers,
Teaching them of their worth.
Healing our bodies, made of dust,
With the Medicine plants that grow,
Reminding each human to honor,
The earthly vehicles of the soul.

Is it time for you to honor the energy you receive from the Earth Mother?
That life force feeds your body. Are you aware of the physical renewal your
body feels when you walk in nature?

THE CLAN CHIEF OF WATER

✄

The shimmering waters reflect
The face of you, who knows,
The feelings of every being who
Has come to Earth to grow.
The Water Spirits sing the song
Of the rivers, seas, and rain,
Of cleansing tears and watery births
That bring new life again.
Clan Chief of Sacred Waters,
You take each flowing form,
You're reflected in the dewdrop,
You dance in the thunderstorm.
You quench the thirst of deserts,
You travel from clouds to sea,
Only to return to the heavens,
As nature's sacred trustee,
You teach us many lessons,
Of how to go with the flow,
Never fighting the currents
That direct the ways we grow.

Have you given thanks for the tears you shed, the water you drink or shower in? The cleansing properties of water allow us to embrace our next level of growth—organically, emotionally, and externally.

THE CLAN CHIEF OF FIRE
✄

You are the molten lava that
Gives the Earth new forms,
You are the lightning bolts,
Crashing through thunderstorms.
You are the human passion
That sets each heart on fire,
Teaching us to create from
Our visions and our desires.
Compassionate fire of Creation,
You keep the Eternal Flame,
That Great Mystery planted
And forever will remain
A constant source of solutions,
For the tests of earthly life,
Teaching each weary pilgrim
That love overcomes the strife.
Your fire lights the Sacred Path,
Allowing our spirits to see,
The constant fire of Creation,
And our infinite longing . . . To be.

Have you been thankful for the sun's warmth, the fire in your heart, or the electric bursts of inspiration that come to you? These are some of the blessings of passionate, fiery creation.

FOGGY MORNING MOUNTAINS
✄

The fog moved silently through the valleys, leaving the mountain-tops free to touch the face of Father Sky. From my viewpoint, I watched the waltz of nature, noting the water-smoke of rolling clouds as they blanketed the lowlands. Here, in the high desert, the rabbit grass had come to full bloom, leaving bright yellow globes of color nestling in the silver-green of the Earth's blanket.

I looked upon the blue-purple ridges that reached high above the clouds. I saw a pair of ravens winging their way to the mountain heights. In the stillness of this winter morning, I saw the two worlds of light and shadow meet and merge.

I wondered what the valley folk would see on this misty morning. Would they look to the sky and feel cheated because there was no sky to see? Or would they trust that somewhere on the high mountaintop, the Winged Creatures still flew and the sun still shone, and that beauty abounded in every part of nature? I realized that the blessing I was being given was seeing both, and honoring each viewpoint as being a glorious part of the whole.

COMMUNICATION
⚒

When we talk with our Relations we are required to know many languages. These varied forms of communication teach us how to use all of our perceptions. We may speak with our human Relations. We can choose to sing or howl with our Creature Relations or just listen to their songs. With our Plant Relations, we are taught to sense their needs and feel their spirits. We can use unspoken language to send our thoughts or feelings to our Ancestors in the Spirit World, and we can voice, sing, or dance our messages of thanksgiving to the Creator. Each form of expression we use is a way of talking, or communicating, that comprises a language of its own.

Every circle of life has its own language. The one language that binds them all together is called Hail-oh-way-an, the Language of Love in the Seneca language. When we approach any creature with love and calmness in our hearts, that creature feels it and will not run. When we sit in silence, filled with joy, we can hear the voices of the Wind Spirits as they move through the trees. If we listen with our hearts, the Water Spirits will sing to us, making their messages known.

Talks with Relations, the Clan Mother of the First Moon Cycle, teaches us how to understand all forms of communication presented by the living beings of the natural world. When is the last time you took a moment to notice if another form of communication was being sent your way? These helpful messages may be intended for our ears only, but unless we become aware of the unique signals life sends, we don't receive any information or any of the spiritual rewards.

TALKS WITH RELATIONS
✄

Mother of Nature talks with her kin.
Stone Person,
*   Wild Flower,*
*   And Wolf are her friend.*

Weaving the rhythms of the seasons,
She rides the Winds of Change,
Opening her heart with gladness,
A shelter from hunger and pain.

Guardian of the needs of Earth,
Making relatives great and small,
Mother, I see you in the dewdrop,
I hear you in the Eagle's call.

Talks with Relations, the Clan Mother of the First Moon Cycle, reminds us that every part of Creation is a potential teacher that mirrors what we need to learn about ourselves. For humankind to expand into the divine human potential, we must begin at the beginning—the Self. We can find the overall pattern of the Great Mystery in every facet of the natural world and see those same patterns within ourselves. The harmony we seek with the world must begin inside. We can make relatives of the warring factions or parts of ourselves that impede our harmony by learning which parts of our human nature oppose one another. Can the jealous part make a Brother of the generous part? Can the insecure part make a Sister of the confident part? Can the male, competitive part marry the female, cooperative part? Try it, and see for yourself how it feels to make happy, unified Relations of the parts of you that are opposed to, or critical of, your other parts.

THE JERICHO ROSE

The wizened old man was a healer of the desert people. He had served his Tribe well and always shared his knowledge freely. One day he was called to doctor a woman who was complaining of sharp, unrelenting belly pains. He went to her lodge, made his prayers, and did the healing. The pain was gone.

Her daughter asked the Old One, "Grandfather, what was that dried up ball of a plant you put on my mother's stomach?"

The old healer smiled as he explained. "That plant is called a Jericho Rose. They blow over the desert like tiny tumbleweeds, naturally uprooting themselves when water is scarce. They then reroot anywhere they happen to be when a rain comes. Daughter, did you notice how the plant opened on your mother's belly when I poured water over it?"

"Why, yes, Grandfather, it was as if the little tumbleweed opened to become a fernlike plant when the water touched it. I noticed that mother's pain left as the plant opened, stopping her moans."

"That is the miracle of the Jericho Rose. It drew the pain out of your mother when its roots sought to reconnect with the earth. Now I will give the plant back to the desert, to be purified by the winds. That plant has served its mission of healing the human beings; we must show our gratitude by giving the Plant Person back its freedom. Like your mother, the Jericho Rose will continue to live, returning another day to serve All Our Relations."

IMMUTABLE LAWS
✄

The immutable, unchangeable laws of nature are based on simple truths:

> Every species insists that only the strong survive so that their species will endure to fulfill specific missions.

> Every pattern in the universe can also be found replicated in nature.

> From the smallest microbacterial world to the largest of all life forms, nothing is ever static; everything always evolves.

> The natural world contains the elements of air, earth, water, fire, and spirit.

If we observe these truths, what natural laws might we find reflected within ourselves?

Could one discovery be that we are being asked to evolve along with the natural world, instead of pretending to be superior to it?

Even in our limited capacity to understand all of the workings of nature, could we possibly discover some truths that are being freely offered?

Could it be time to pay closer attention?

EARTH ELEMENTS

We live in air, but we do not see it, forgetting to show our thanks for the breath that gives us life.

Our bodies are made of the elements of earth, but few recognize the essential energy of the Earth Mother that fuels our physical strength.

Water blends our dreams and feelings into a sacred creative drive called the will, but few have learned to master freewill or the flow of Creation.

Our hearts contain fire, the Eternal Flame of Love, but few have learned how to use its light to illuminate their paths.

These elements give us the ability to touch our primal human natures and the potential of our spirits, seeing both as being equally sacred.

These questions arise: How did we stray so far from the basic wisdom of the Earth Mother and the Great Mystery? Was it too simple a set of truths? Or did our intellectual judgments infuse us with a disdain for earthly experiences as being less desirable than spiritual concepts? When flesh, mind, spirit, *and will* meet inside a human form, it is Divine Creation at its best!

FALSE OWNERSHIP
✂

The Earth Mother belongs to herself and has always reclaimed every part of her soil. The false sense of ownership has been defended by countless civilizations that fought over self-declared borders, killing other humans in order to possess verdant valleys or wide savannas. Mother Earth is a living organism that can never be owned by anyone.

The ages of ice have all but obliterated the ancient remains of hundreds of vanished peoples. The ice age will come again when the Wheel of Life turns. It may not come for another thousand years, but it will happen. Knowing this, doesn't it seem foolish for humankind to waste life force and resources to proclaim ownership rather than healing the separation created by fear or greed?

Talks with Relations, the Clan Mother of the First Moon Cycle, reminds us that the family of humankind could change the ideas of false ownership with this personal commitment:

> *Earth Mother, let me show gratitude,*
> *For the abundance you freely give,*
> *By pledging to be a caretaker,*
> *Respecting all things that live.*
>
> *Great Mystery, hear my solemn decree,*
> *And guide me in these ways,*
> *That I may honor my Mother,*
> *With a heart that's full of praise.*

REVERIE OF AWARENESS

Mountain Ram kept butting his head against the tree, nearly shaking the nest containing Blue Bird's family out of the branches. Blue Bird, being very upset, chattered angrily at Mountain Ram. Ram looked up with glazed eyes, trying to focus on who had been yelling at him. He was ashamed. His head cleared and he explained that he had been angry, banging his rage into the tree.

After listening to Ram's tale of woe, Blue Bird became gentle with her Four-legged brother. She told him that the language of rage always lashed out at the unsuspecting, making others a wrong target.

Blue Bird, the Keeper of Happiness, explained that Ram had forgotten what gave him joy. He had allowed his anger at being forced into another territory by his herd's dominant male to kill his sense of adventure. Instead of looking for the opportunities in his new territory, he had used his anger to hurt himself and to threaten others.

Ram regained his happiness by remembering his own Medicine of surefootedness and the ability to overcome the treachery of new paths. The reverie of this new awareness made him appreciate the adventure he could encounter in the turn of his life's events.

Is it time for you to see what kind of things make you happy? If you notice what makes you unhappy, you may find that each unhappy moment also gives you an opportunity to create a new path that leads out of stagnation and into adventure.

INTIMACY WITH THE NATURAL WORLD
✖

The Red Race has lived in intimacy with the natural world for all time. Those who still live with nature, in the manner that creates this intimate bond, can taste the wind and monitor the migrations of the creatures. These human beings notice every subtle change in the atmosphere, the way a sensitive woman knows and responds to her lover's hands. There is no separation between the movements of the natural world and the sensory responses invoked in a human being who has come to this intimate understanding of Oneness.

If we learn to trust our senses and to respond to the quiet input of those messages in our consciousness, we can perceive countless subtle indications of change. This kind of intimacy is a valued skill, learned through many trial-and-error experiences. When we master the responses inside of ourselves, learning to trust our senses, the languages of unspoken inner knowing come alive. This skill can be applied to all areas of our lives. The key to achieving this type of inner awareness comes through intimacy. When we are intimately connected with every reaction and response inside our bodies, while being totally still and silent, new worlds open to us. Is it time for you to trust the responses of your perceptions?

THE LANGUAGE OF CURIOSITY
✂

Curiosity is a language
   That has many goals,
Opening the human mind
   And the searching soul.

The art of discovery,
   Adventure on the trail,
The unexpected allusions,
   The lure to prevail.

When does the seeker tire
   Of questing through the unknown?
Is it when we lose the fire
   Of learning what's been shown?

Buried treasure lurks nearby,
In curiosity's goal.
The wealth of wisdom is unveiled,
Enrichment for the soul.

Is it time to reclaim your excitement and curiosity about learning what our world has to offer?

THE EARTH BLANKET
✖

The Tribe of all things green and growing speaks to us in many ways. The Plant People and Standing People (trees) are good role models for their human Relations. It is through this green and growing Tribe that we can learn the lessons of balanced giving and receiving, generosity, interdependence, and standing tall.

This Tribe of the Plant Kingdom is called the Earth Blanket. It not only blankets the Earth Mother, but it gives sheltering homes to all other life forms. The Earth Blanket recycles the air we breathe and the water we drink. Without this blanket, we would not survive.

Most of the natural cures for human diseases are found in the forests and rain forests of our planet. It would be a shame to lose all human life to plagues because the cures for those diseases were no longer available, the forests having been destroyed to make throw-away chopsticks. In Brazil, six hundred acres a day are destroyed for that usage alone. Our Plant Relations carry many keys to our survival as a planet; can we afford to be so ignorant or so wasteful?

To cut a living tree without that Standing Person's permission is to destroy a living being. Ask yourself how you would feel if it were your child being cut down. Then you will know the pain the Plant Kingdom feels and the horror this strikes into the hearts of those of us who can hear their screams.

SACRED SPACE
✖

The forest creatures were speaking to one another and conversing with the plants when an old man and a little girl began making their way up the trail that led to the alpine meadow. Everyone noticed that these humans were reverent as they passed through the various glens that were connected by the elk trails. This quiet and respectful behavior made the forest Relations happy, showing that some humans understood and honored the Sacred Spaces of other life forms.

When the two humans reached the alpine meadow, the little girl asked her Grandfather if she had observed the Sacred Spaces of her Relations properly, causing him to grin when he nodded his pleasure at her behavior. The little one then asked her Grandfather where Sacred Space lived. After trying to blink back the tears of tenderness in his eyes, he spoke.

"Little One, each living thing's Sacred Space lives in between the in breath and the out breath. We cannot always see its outer boundaries, but the center of its home is nestled in the space between two heartbeats."

SEEING THE OVERVIEW
⚟

The feathered friends, which the Ancestors called Winged-ones, teach humankind many lessons. These birds, who bring us a calliope of songs that thrill our hearts and ears, have one great message in common for the human race. They teach us to let go of our tunnel vision and to look at our lives from a perspective that gives us the overview.

When overwhelm sets in and we are pounded by details, keeping us from our balanced perspective, we can find a solution. The human imagination allows us to pretend we are flying above our present situation. From this vantage point, the overall pattern of life takes on a new meaning. The Winged-ones are our Allies in this process of untangling the knots. Just as the birds weave bits of twigs and strings into their nests, we sometimes get so lost in creating our nests that we forget where we started and where our close-up observation was supposed to end. Unraveling the mess we created, through being too self-absorbed, can be accessed by seeing the overview from the skies above. Fly high and really look at the perimeters of your creation!

Talks with Relations, the Clan Mother of the First Moon Cycle, asks us to take a break and to imagine the overview. By noticing the horizon, the overall patterns, and the many paths in and out of the landscape, we can bring order to chaos.

LISTENING TO LEARN
✖

A meeting was going on in the forest. The Creature-beings were trying to sort out the problems caused by the latest migrations of their
northern neighbors that were affecting their food supply. The Great
Ice Mountains made it necessary for the northern Relations to flee
the cold of encroaching glaciers, forcing them into the territories of
these concerned forest dwellers.

Magpie was chattering away while the other creatures listened
to her recent experiences. Rabbit then added his point of view, complaining about having to ask the newcomers to respect the needs of
creatures who had always lived in this forest. Chipmunk piped up
and reminded the others to focus on solutions that would allow
everyone to be fed. Fox and Wolf agreed, each adding a solution,
while Squirrel gathered all the information.

Bluejay noticed that Bear had not said a thing. Finally, Bluejay
asked Bear why she was so silent, and Bear replied, "I'm listening
and learning. I don't need to talk; *I already know what I know.*"

REFLECTIONS OF THE SKY NATION
✂

The Thunder-beings were busy giving birth to new clouds, sending them to dance in the blue playground of sky. Grandfather Sun provided the glittering sunbeams, which acted like jump ropes for today's newborn white, puffy Cloud People.

One of the most curious little clouds wandered off on the winds. She decided she was going to have a talk with Sacred Mountain. "Grandmother Mountain, I've come to ask you if your forests need rain today," she said. "I want to be of service, and so I thought I had better find out what is needed most."

Sacred Mountain told the little cloud that there was plenty of moisture today, but the little one could help in another way. Sacred Mountain taught the little cloud how to understand the thoughts and questions that the human beings were having. It was fun for the little cloud to capture the waves of human thoughts rising from the Earth and to answer the humans' unspoken questions by becoming shapes that formed a series of ideas. The needed answers were found through linking ideas.

The little cloud approached Sacred Mountain at the end of the day with another question that caused Cloud to have a heavy heart, "Grandmother Mountain, I've worked all day to reflect helpful answers to the Human Tribe, but now I have one very important question. How can we get them to look up and pay attention?"

2ND
MOON

SEEKING WISDOM
✖

Those who do not seek the wisdom of their Elders are blinded by stubbornness, self-importance, and their own folly.

Human beings cannot see all of the potential solutions or the possible results of their actions when they are angry, confused, or in pain.

The Great Mystery, Maker of All Things, has given each human being the opportunity to grow beyond limitation through experiencing the challenges of the tangible world. Those who have bested the struggles and sorrows, continuing to love life and all human beings, are the Wisdom Keepers. Seeking advice from these faithful Two-leggeds opens one's path to healing and personal growth.

Wisdom Keeper is the Clan Mother of the Second Moon Cycle who reminds us that every human being has gifts of wisdom. Whether those skills are developed depends upon the person's willingness to look at other points of view. When we are open to change and learning from others, we are asking for personal growth. When we insist upon being the sole authority on any subject, we show the world our fear of change and our stubborn self-importance.

Humans can mask their insecurity in many ways. The sure signs are self-importance, addictions, stubbornness, the need to be right, and the refusal to ask for help or advice.

TWISTING THE WISDOM
✄

Some will deny the wisdom presented because of their ignorance. Others will protect their need to be the only carriers of truth by trying to discredit any other messenger who shares knowledge freely. Those in fear of change may attack the truths of their own Ancestors, and the greedy will twist the truth to serve their own ends.

These children of sorrow cannot see the truth or hear the wisdom because the pain and anger have blinded them and stopped up their ears. They may seek to destroy the credibility of the messenger, but the message of truth will endure.

Wisdom Keeper, the Clan Mother of the Second Moon Cycle, reminds us that we all must answer to one Source, the Creator of All Life. This Source is the only authority. Human beings and human-made laws pale in the light of the Creator.

The ultimate question of intent is answered in the heart of the individual. Those with the courage to ask this question, requiring truth from the core of the Self, have found the pathways to healing the shadowy sides of their natures.

CREATING A SAFE SPACE
✂

Some people have a talent
For creating Sacred Space;
Where others feel the comfort,
Natural safety they embrace.
Welcomed by the openness,
Where no judgments reside,
The implicit trust of feeling
In a heart that's opened wide.
This rare living treasure
Is a confidant and friend,
Whose honor is impeccable,
On whose word we can depend.
This person is a Wisdom Keeper
Who defends every Sacred Space,
Through loyalty and acceptance,
The remembered gifts of grace.

One of the greatest gifts of Wisdom Keeper, the Clan Mother of the Second Moon Cycle, to humankind is the understanding of nonthreatening, safe space. Learning to honor the truth has many ways to teach us about authentic friendship. When we create a safe space for others, we have tapped the Remembering, which teaches us that the external safe space we can create for others reflects our internal safe space, which has eliminated negative judgments. Is it time to look at someone you know who has these gifts and use that person as your role model?

THE DANCE OF THE REMEMBERING
❌

"What is the Remembering, Grandmother?" the young woman asked.

And the Wise One replied, "The Remembering is many things, because it is a gradual unfoldment of the Spiritual Essence. The Remembering takes form when human beings come fully alert, aware of all that has come before, their rightful place in Creation, and choice of paths the Great Mystery gave them. Then the Ancestor Spirits tell the awakened humans how to accomplish their tasks in life through the use of their own good Medicine. The Spiritual Essence, the Orenda, speaks to the person through the heart's desire, and the human being remembers more.

"When the Remembering comes, human beings are caught in a spiral that mirrors the flight of Grouse, constantly spiraling upward through the many Wheels of Life, bringing wisdom. Through these lessons, the personal understanding grows, connecting these people in Oneness to the whole of Creation. They can never turn back after that moment, because their lives are changed forever."

SNOWFLAKES
✖

Snowflakes hold the patterns of our dreams and desires inside their frozen Medicine Wheels. Our thoughts and aspirations are alive and contain spirit. Like wisps of smoke in a snowstorm, the spirit contained in our dreams takes form, fashioning the unique patterns in each snowflake.

The frozen mound of collected dreams that form the glistening, white crowns of majestic mountains return to us in spring to feed all living things. The melted waters of the Snowflake Clan teach us to drink deeply of the sweet dreams that through mingling create harmony and nurture all of Creation until the end of time.

Wisdom Keeper, Clan Mother of the Second Moon Cycle, teaches us to share our dreams with one another, to open our visions to those who can share in the Remembering. When we share the goodness of what we remember from our personal dreams, we learn to piece together the shards of the Earth Mother's dream, which is Life abundant for all living things.

ANCIENT KNOWING
✂

The wisdom of the Ancients
Floats upon the seas,
Nestles in the forests,
And stands among the trees.
This ancient form of knowing,
Grows amidst the sands,
Waiting for the human race
To learn from the land.
There among the whispers,
Of creatures, stones, and wind,
The wisdom of the Ancestors
Is waiting to befriend
Any human seeker who
Wants to find the way,
Honoring the ancient wisdom
Through actions taken today.

Application is everything. When wisdom is spoken from the intellect but not integrated into behavior it carries no clout. Is it time for you to live the wisdom, instead of intellectually espousing what you believe is correct behavior for the enlightened?

HOSPITALITY

In the Indian community, hospitality has always been a Tradition that is founded on the deepest respect humans can show one another. Any person hosting another is required to sponsor that person and to be responsible for that person's actions while they are a guest in the host's land. Being a guest requires that one observe all of the customs and Traditions of the place where they are visiting.

The guest is expected to behave with respect toward the host family, to contribute by helping with the work at hand, to follow the customs of that land, to honor the Ancestors, Ceremonies, and spirits of that area, and to be grateful for the hospitality offered. If possible, the guest should help provide anything that is needed—gifts of food that will feed the host family are always welcome.

If every human being saw the homes and lands that they visited as being the Sacred Space of someone else who was willing to vouch for the behavior of the guest, they would understand the special respect, trust, and opportunity being offered. To be flippant or disrespectful, or to take hospitality for granted, is a sign of ignorance. The wise person sees the gift being offered, respects the opportunity, accepts with gratitude, and gives back by taking on the same responsibilities as the other family members without having to be asked.

HOPE AND TRUST

In the heart where hope is present,
There burns a living fire,
Shedding light upon the future,
Fanning it with desire.
Hope stands with one door open,
Inviting the seeker inside,
But cannot chase away the doubts
Or the fears where they hide.

Trust comes when we seekers
Have asked to be blessed,
Have accepted the courage given,
As a gift of our quests.
Then having inner knowing,
With Great Mystery by our sides,
We trust that when we get there,
Every door will open wide.

THE FAITHFUL
✖

The little child asked her blind Grandmother who the Faithful were, and the Old One's cloudy eyes were suddenly lit from within. A look of longing danced across her wood-grainy features as she began to speak.

"The Faithful are the human beings who can hear our Earth Mother's voice. They are the Two-leggeds who treat every living thing with respect. They carry the Remembering. These human beings understand the Earth, they remember who they are and why they are here, and they have accepted the roles of guardianship. They are called the Faithful because they have followed the Red Road of Faith. Through seeking the ancient wisdom of the Remembering, they have discovered that faith is a sacred trust: a bond between the Great Mystery, the Earth Mother, and the individual.

"Long ago, when I was blinded, my heart held rage. I felt abandoned by the Creator. Through many long months of anger and tears, I was taught to see again. No, my child, it was not with these cloudy eyes. I learned that through acceptance of Great Mystery's plan, I could trust my path—even in my personal darkness. I began to see pictures in my mind's eye, and I was not alone; the Faithful welcomed me into the Circle of Life. I learned to trust the Earth Mother's voice, I learned to honor all of my senses, and I had faith in the wisdom I carry. These are the gifts given to the Faithful, honoring the truth with gratitude. I am grateful for my blindness because it has taught me faith, and with my faith, I can see."

THE INDICATOR
✖

For many hundreds of years, Indian people have used their eyes and chins to indicate what they wanted another to look at. If one observes closely, it is easy to discern where a person is putting their attention. The discreet person directs his or her eyes to the location and then gently nods the head up, pointing with the chin. This practice is a sign of good manners as well as a way to keep a personal conversation fairly private. Pointing with the chin is not as common in modern culture because most people are not paying close attention to another who is speaking, consequently, the subtlety is lost on an inattentive listener.

My wise Grandmother, Yewenode, taught me that people should never point a finger at others, because when we do, three fingers are pointing back at us!

WISDOM OF THE WARRIOR CLAN
✖

A MAN WITHOUT MEASURE IS A MAN
WHO HAS KNOWINGLY BROKEN THE
WARRIORS' VOW.

The Warriors' Vow is to protect the Elders, Life Givers, and children with strength, courage, support, and wisdom until his last breath. In Indian Tradition, any man who knowingly does anything to hurt women, children, or Elders is considered worthless and loses his standing as a Warrior.

In ancient times, a man who raped or molested anyone would be killed. Any member of the Warrior Clan who stole anything or told lies was disgraced, banished, or put to death, depending upon the severity of his dishonesty.

Any man who would run a Purification Ceremony with Elders, women, and children present—running it hot, like a Warriors' sweat—could hurt the People. Any man who resorted to violence or emotional abuse was not a Warrior. Any man who stooped to arguments with Elders, women, or children was not upholding his vow to the People. These values still hold true, but few are strong enough to embrace the vow without faltering or making mistakes.

CLOUD PEOPLE
✕

A little boy stood watching the changes in the sky while his father finished making an arrowhead.

"Father, why is it that I see the Cloud People's faces in the sky and then they change?"

"The Cloud People are telling you a story, my son. Shall we watch and figure out the Medicine Story the Sky Nation is giving you today?"

As the two watched, they saw the giant profile face of a man, made of clouds, with his lips pursed as if he was whistling or blowing air. Then it changed. An Eagle appeared to be gliding on the currents. Later, another change brought the lone figure of an Indian warrior, reaching for an arrow that was flying across the sky. The arrow changed to an eagle feather, and the clouds rolled away.

After reflecting, the boy explained that he saw the Wind Chief blow the breeze that lifted Eagle's wings. The warrior on the ground had to reach higher than his head to catch the arrow of truth. In grasping that truth, the warrior earned an eagle feather. The warrior became the brother of Eagle, understanding the truth that Great Mystery sent through his spiritual messengers of the Sky Nation.

STONE PEOPLE
✄

Sacred libraries etched in stone,
Please help me find my way;
Symbols of all the Earth has known,
Mark the language you display.
Can I read your alphabet,
And will I understand,
The silent message you send me,
While resting in my hands?
Will I grasp the meanings,
Of the steps I must take,
To walk with you in beauty,
As my spirit comes awake?
And is the warmth you send
An understanding alive in me,
Reflected by Earth Mother,
And the Sacred Mystery?
Will you open the Remembering,
I feel sleeping inside of me?
Do you know my deepest longing
To be all that I can be?
Silent messenger of the Earth,
My teacher made of stone,
I honor your seeds of wisdom
And the knowing you have sown.

SACRED PATH STONE

The warrior was running through the woods making his way home from carrying a message to another band of his Nation. It was his task to relay the other Chief's response without changing any of the message's content—memorizing the words, the cadence, and emulating the honor being returned to his Elders.

Along the way, he tripped upon a stone, falling into the brambles. In his disgust with himself, he nearly hurled the stone into the forest before he noticed that the rock had a wide line of another color running through its center. He knew that there was a reason for the Earth Mother putting this Stone Person in his path. He greeted the stone, placed it in the palm of his left hand, and continued on his way.

After delivering his message with ease, the warrior went to the Holy Man, who told him of the Stone Person's Medicine. The warrior learned that any stone with a line of another color all the way through it carried the Medicine of focus, stamina, determination, and persistence. This Sacred Path Stone showed humans how to follow the Beauty Way. The stone taught humankind to have the courage to stay on the path of peace, being kind messengers who carry Good Medicine.

THE TREES ARE TEACHERS
✖

The trees are called Standing People because they are our teachers. They do not walk about like human beings, but they do hold the energy of Earth and Sky. The roots of the trees go deep into our Mother Earth, and their branches reach for the sunlight high in the sky. These teachers of the woods show humankind how to balance the male and female energies present in every human being. Through their example, we can learn how to give and receive. The trees are firmly grounded in the Earth and are reaching for the heavens with their branches, showing human beings how to be bridges between the tangible and nontangible worlds. The balance of demonstrative and receptive is found in the heart of humans and in the trunk of the trees.

These living examples of balance allow humankind to discover the flow of life force that brings inner peace. It is circular and flows up through the roots to the top of the branches, traveling down to the roots again, creating a recycling of energy.

Wisdom Keeper, the Clan Mother of the Second Moon Cycle, reminds us that when we can see the energy coursing through our bodies, like the circular flow of the trees being fed by the Earth, we can find balance. When we accomplish this task, we no longer leak, waste, or misuse our energy because it is constantly being recycled.

WISDOM KEEPER
⚏

Oh keeper of ancient knowing,
Whisper your wisdom to me,
That I may always remember
Life's sacred mystery.

The stories of the Grandmothers,
Brave deeds great and small,
The progress of the Faithful,
Who answer our Mother's call.

The cycles and the seasons
That mark our every change,
The rebirth of our visions,
The spirit we have reclaimed.

Here truth is the victor
Of the war that dwells within,
Bringing every human heart
To celebration in the end.

Wisdom Keeper, Clan Mother of the Second Moon Cycle, asks us to clear the path to remembering by weeding out all of the past events that hold our attention. In order to reclaim the fragments of our spirits that remain stuck in old traumas, disappointments, and heartaches, we must breathe these lost pieces of Self free from the feelings we forgot to express at the time. In this manner, we free our energy, reclaim the vision we owned before our disappointment, and bring that shard of ourselves home—to the present. Then we have all the attention and focus we need to be in the Now, remembering who we are and why we are here.

THE DESICCATING POWER OF SELF-DOUBT
✵

To DOUBT THE WISDOM OF ONE'S OWN EXPERIENCE
IS TO REDUCE THE RIVERS OF LIFE TO AN ARID DESERT.
TO GIVE AWAY THE VALIDITY AND AUTHORITY
OF PERSONAL EXPERIENCE, BY DEFERRING TO A
SELF-PROCLAIMED EXPERT, IS TO DEHYDRATE THE
FLOWS OF CREATION THAT NATURALLY COURSE
THROUGH ALL PEOPLE WHO HONOR THEIR PERSONAL
FEELINGS AND TRUTHS.

In a world that contains as many personal truths as there are people, it is often difficult to maintain integrity with the Self. It is perfectly okay to agree to disagree with another. Personal experience differs greatly from person to person. We all carry personal likes and dislikes. Being true to the Self and trusting one's own feelings and perceptions without deception is an art. When we master this art, we feel alive and at one with the flow of life. When we negate our abilities to honor our personal truths with self-doubt, we find the flow of life drying up before our eyes. To question is healthy. To deny the feelings found in truthful answers is to doubt the foundation of being—the will.

If self-doubt is creating confusion, you may want to try this solution of Wisdom Keeper's, Clan Mother of the Second Moon Cycle: To open the flood gates again, rehydrating the oasis of inner knowing that you carry, simply recall where you deferred to another, denying the truth of your personal experience—then, reclaim your authority.

THE FIRST SNOW
∝

The leaves were still raging with color when the first snow came to the silent mountains of the Earth Mother. Looking down from the Spirit World, Wisdom Keeper breathed a sigh of relief, having feared that the human beings had forgotten the importance of dreaming. The appearance of the snowflakes, which held the patterns of human hopes and aspirations in their frozen wheels, temporarily relieved the Medicine Guardian of her fears.

The Wise One remembered that less and less snow had come during the last few winters, and this realization troubled her. Were her human children forgetting to use their imaginations? Were they so busy that they had lost the will to recapture their innocence and wonder of life? Had the false masks of sophistication robbed them of their common destiny? She knew that the destiny of humankind was to remember who they were and to use their talents to dream the coming World of Peace.

She sighed as she wondered how many would grasp the double meanings of the Remembering. Had separation robbed her children of picking up the fragments of themselves and *re-membering* themselves into wholeness? Could the Two-legged Tribe of humans access their connections to the Great Mystery and claim the awareness that was their right?

She knew the answer. Not without imagination, daring, freewill, and the power of the dreamer. She also knew that all she could do was assist those who sought her out—and *to trust that the dreamers would awaken.*

RESPECTING DANGER
✖

The wise person respects the potential dangers found in the wild. The arctic glaciers and blinding snows have their own ways of insisting upon respect. The deserts of the Earth Mother can render a person senseless and dehydrated, forgetting the presence of rattling sidewinders and other deadly creatures. The sudden storms on the oceans, the tornadoes of the plains, the raging floods of monsoons, and the rumbles of earthquakes all demand that the danger signals be taken seriously. Weather can be deadly.

Human beings have learned throughout time to use good judgment and primitive instinct if they want to survive. Our modern world has added a new set of dangers, the unseen killers of radiation and pollution. Crime and violence have destroyed the lives of many. The spiritual, sexual, physical, and emotional dangers of abuse have also taken countless tolls on humanity's well-being.

Is the lack of self-respect the reason that humans have not quite learned how to recognize these dangers and correct them? Or is it the hopelessness that keeps humans from removing themselves from harm's way? The solutions are not simple. The basic building block of recovering our wisdom and humanity is always the same. Respect for all life. Respect for the Self. No set of solutions can flourish without basic integrity and respect for all parts of Creation. If we lose touch with the ability to respect all life, we have given our authority and our permission for degradation and danger to reign.

MODESTY
✖

Modesty has always been considered a desirable quality and attribute in the Native American community. Any people who blow their own horns, talk loudly or excessively, or make a spectacle of themselves are looked upon as being very out of balance.

Those who have done well or have earned acknowledgment through their actions, being publicly recognized, have brought honor to the community. These people are appreciated to the degree that they have accepted their public status with modesty—leaving any ego outside of the lodges of our People. When visiting their families or visiting another Native American community, these gifted ones find it necessary to return with their humility, sense of equality, and spiritual values intact. If not, they will be called to a Circle, to speak with the Elders about correcting their inappropriate, self-important attitudes.

Wisdom Keeper, Clan Mother of the Second Moon Cycle, shows us the value of modesty when she reminds us that all people who call attention to themselves by acting superior are really very wounded or insecure. When people can be modest about their accomplishments and work with others as equals, they have learned the value of communicating in unity. In accepting every person as being equally valuable to the whole, we learn that the foundations of any culture cannot be sustained unless every building block that supports the whole is honored.

KEEPERS OF EARTH MEDICINE

✂

Mother Earth sighed with pleasure because more human beings were learning to respect the ancient ways that supported harmony. She could feel the commitment of her human children who had passed many tests in order to take their roles as Keepers of Earth Medicine. As she placed her attention on the Ceremony that was being held to honor the new Guardians, happiness flooded into her being. She watched her human children as the Ceremony proceeded.

The men and women who were the newest Keepers of Earth Medicine stood in a Circle around a blazing fire, their faces lit from within, as well as from the radiant firelight. The Elders accepted each person's pledge to uphold Life, Unity, and Equality for Eternity. The head male and female Elders stood back-to-back, the male Elder speaking to the female side of the circle and the female Elder speaking to the men's side. The balance was created as the Wise Ones spoke their final proclamation in unison, reminding the new Guardians of the solemn responsibilities they now held for all of humanity.

"You are becoming the Guardians of the Sacred Traditions of the Ancestors. You have been taught these ways and were given this wisdom as a gift. Honor these ways with all that you are, and each of you will become both the past and the future. *Soil them, and the past will give you no future.*"

THE SELFLESS SERVANT

The selfless servant remembers
The challenges along the way,
But meets each Sun with wonder,
The pleasure of greeting the day.
The joy that fuels the selfless heart
Is in seeing the changes that come
To every weary traveler who hears
The heart song of Earth Mother's drum.
Affecting the lives of those in need,
With a smile or a helping hand,
Brings unseen rewards to the heart
That the selfish don't understand.
Returning to others a percentage
Of the abundance that we have known
Is the sacred wisdom of sharing,
A gift of the seeds we have sown.
Where do we find these servants,
Who choose to selflessly give?
They stand with Wisdom Keeper,
Having remembered,

   that to give is to live!

REMEMBERING THE EARTHWALK
⚒

The figure of the wizened old man silently waited at his campfire in the Spirit World, anticipating the arrival of a young spirit who was preparing to take a human form. The young one bounced toward the fire, showing his self-importance by strutting from one side of the fire to the other. When he finally stopped his puffed-up prancing, the Ancient One began to speak.

"So, you are going to fall from the sky and nestle in the womb of an earth woman. There are many things there that will be peculiar to you. The human beings are a curious mix of thoughts and feelings. It will take you a while to adjust to the perils of an Earthwalk. The challenges are many. You may encounter the loss of loved ones, defeats in battle, the heartaches of broken dreams, or the cruelty of humankind toward one another."

The old one grunted, "Umph, yes, you could get lost. Better to tell you of the other things that help humans find themselves. The pleasures of love, the joys of children, the beauty of nature, the depth of the heart's feelings—these things are there, too. You will have to learn how to balance all of the Earthwalk's experiences and lessons."

Being full of himself and his upcoming new adventure, the young one's voice was arrogant when he spoke, "It sounds like a hard road, Grandfather. Maybe *you* will find the strength to try it when *your* chance arrives."

The Old One replied, "So, you are hiding *your* fear behind that false bravado, humh! Your silly foolishness amuses me! I'm no coward; *I was human once!*"

THE WAY OF WISDOM
><

THE MORE THAT PEOPLE LEARN AND
THE MORE WISDOM THEY GATHER,
THE MORE SURE THEY BECOME THAT
THEY KNOW NOTHING. THIS PROCESS
IS CALLED THE WAY OF WISDOM.

If you are unsure about others' statements about themselves, the surest way to size them up is to ask several difficult questions. If at any time, they say that they do not know the answer, you will discover that they carry the quality of sincerity. The know-it-alls won't admit they don't have all the answers. The con artists will make up the answers. The pseudo-intellectuals will try to confuse you with complex concepts that cannot be sanely understood. The strategists will try to divert your attention to another area. The bottom line is a simple, honest admission: "Gee, I don't know."

The wise person understands that when others are not listening, or are having to know all the answers, they create their own debilitating barriers to learning.

RESPONDING TO THE CALL
✣

Medicine Crow sat in his lodge and waited. He knew someone special was coming today. His dreams had told him that this person would be a great help to the People, even though the man had been raised in a different culture.

It did not surprise the Holy Man when one of the settlers, who lived nearby, rode up on a horse. Medicine Crow remembered this one; he liked him. The man had defended a member of the Tribe against unjust accusations a few moons back. When the young man had smoked a Pipe with the Old One, they spoke.

"I have come to ask for your wise advice, Medicine Crow. I feel that I am being called to be a bridge between our cultures. You have shown me the good hearts of your Tribe, and I want to be of service. I want to teach my race how to respect your culture, so I went to the minister of our church for advice. All he said was, 'Many are called, but few are chosen.' I don't understand what he meant."

The young settler was taken aback when Medicine Crow started laughing and rolling on the ground. The old one was guffawing so much, he cried. When the Wise One could finally speak again, he replied, "I see now why we think your race is so curiously backward sometimes. In our Teachings we say, 'All are called and chosen, but few listen or find the courage to take action!'"

WISDOM AS FEELING

Some people work very hard trying to figure out the workings of the Great Mystery and life. These seekers of ultimate truth have been taught to think in lines rather than to feel and perceive in Circles. The Creator is the Great Mystery, the All-Unfolding.

How arrogant is the human species? Do we truly believe that we must label and make lists of our limited, human understandings of Creation in order to claim the knowledge of the profound simplicity of truth?

As we commune with the natural world, we feel the All as it is unfolding because the All touches every part of our beingness with the Great Mystery's most passionate desire to continue creating life abundant.

Wisdom is often felt and perceived rather than intellectualized. The simple wisdom of honoring all of the body's senses can open new worlds to those who have forgotten to feel the celebration of life. Whether the numbness comes from the unwillingness to heal old pain or from the fear of scarcity, the result is the same. Human beings forget the simple blessings of watching a sunrise or listening for the nightingale's song in the starry night. In this state of unawareness, we lose our connections to the Earth Mother's wisdom—forgetting how good it is to be alive!

DEVELOPING THE SELF
✖

The Self's desire to develop
Hidden talents and unused skills
Comes when we remember
The freedom of reclaimed will.
Former confusion and laziness
Will vanish without a strain,
Replaced with passionate desire,
The remembered Self contains.
The excitement of discovery,
Awakened feelings of delight,
Imagination scouts the trail,
Spreading our wings for flight.
Recollections fuel the fire,
The development is our own,
In this Eagle's Rite of Passage,
We earn our freedom—
  by learning to fly alone.

Developing the human potential is accessed through the Remembering.
When something happens, sparking our desire to grow, to change, or to
develop our talents, Great Mystery's intervention is at hand. When people
awaken to their potential, they begin Eagle's Rite of Passage. This initia-
tion process forces us to leave the nest, or comfort zone. We begin by de-
veloping our talents with the assistance of others, until we can fly solo.
With solo flight, we have come to trust ourselves; that earned trust in the
Self is freedom.

OFFERS KINDNESS

The woman scrubbed herself with sand at the river's edge. After a long winter, the sand washing felt good as the layers of dead skin rolled off the soles of her feet. Lost in her thoughts, she did not notice anything amiss until she heard a little girl crying. Looking up, she saw the child's stepmother scrubbing the child's skin raw; it was bleeding.

In a heartbeat, she was on her feet, running through the water. Whisking the crying child from the stepmother's grasp, she rocked the little girl, whispering to her, and then handed the child to one of the other women. Without any anger, she softly spoke to the erring woman.

"Turkey Feather, I understand how hard it has been for you to raise my deceased sister's child. She was your old rival, the first wife to your husband. I will speak to her father who once was my brother. He will understand if I lighten your burden by taking the child to my lodge to live."

Turkey Feather spat at the ground and used a hand sign to indicate she was done with both of them forever, then stormed off. The woman watched her retreat, thinking of how much effort it must take to be that hurtful. She turned back to the river and made the blessing sign with her hand, showing her gratitude to the Creator for her own Medicine and her name—Offers Kindness.

3RD
MOON

WEIGHS THE TRUTH
✖

The Clan Mother of the Third Moon Cycle is the Protectress of the Underdog and Keeper of Equality. She reminds us that when we judge anything or anyone in our lives, we have lost the balance found in personal harmony.

The truth is never in black-and-white. There are usually more than two sides to every question. There are usually as many truths as people or situations involved. The truth has many facets and shapes, comes in many forms. Every living thing has a Sacred Point of View and is given the right to express that truth through the way that life is lived.

Weighs the Truth reminds us that life is a myriad of feelings that teach us what feels good and what feels bad. From these personal feelings, we learn to hear the small, still voice within our hearts. This inner voice speaks from our Spiritual Essences and will not accept justifications of the mind. This place of balance inside us is immune to greed, malice, and jealousy. From the center of our Sacred Spaces come our abilities to weigh the truth without prejudice. Once found, this voice will always prevail. Healing the battle scars of human life, which keep us deaf to the sacred voice of truth, is the first step toward accepting the magnitude of our human potential.

Are you ready to accept the gentle voice of your Sacred Self that will teach you how to find the path to personal truth?

WEIGHING THE TRUTH
✄

The little boy was angry. His feelings were hurt, his vision clouded by pain. His Grandfather stopped him from running alone to the woods and spoke to the child, listening to his tale of woe.

The little warrior held a stone his Grandfather had given him, feeling its weight. Another stone, and yet another, was added until the child finally nodded. This was the weight the little boy felt was equal to his pain.

The wise Grandfather told the child that the weight of the stones would equal the burden the boy would have to carry for all of his days if he were not willing to find a way to give it away. The little brave finally allowed himself to be held, letting the salty tears release and cleanse his pain. Grandfather's strong arms comforted him, and the weight of the burden was lifted. The clouds rolled from the little one's vision, and he could see the value of turning to the ones he loved, sharing his burden—so that he would not have to carry it for all of the winters of his Earthwalk.

MALICE

Malice wounds the human heart
That sends its hateful pain,
Numbs the senses of the soul,
And causes the body to wane.
Malice is born of envy,
With jealousy at its side,
Companions of greed and avarice,
In the hardened heart reside.
Fear stalks the one who uses
Malice as a weapon in life,
Slaying all good intentions,
Losing the war of inner strife.
Bitterness wages the battle
Within that troubled mind,
Riddled with fears of conquest,
The bigotry of humankind.
The wedge of separation has
Split the body, mind, and soul,
Blinding us to healing solutions,
That could make each person whole.

Where within human misery,
Can malice be allowed to die,
Changing all the judgments
That fostered "an eye for an eye"?
Must unity come through disasters,
Making separation disappear,
Leaving all Earth's children
The common bond of tears?
Or are we ready to let go
Of the inherited malice we bring,
Unhealed parts of our woundedness,
And the fears to which we cling?

HONESTY
✂

Honesty is one of the four characteristics that Medicine People look for when they observe others who may have leadership potential. If a young candidate shows integrity through always being truthful, he or she may be rewarded by the Elders. One of the rewards of honesty is having further wisdom passed to those who deserve and revere it. The mysteries of nature, the Spirit World, and the healing arts can be discussed, but the sacred experience of having these visions has to be earned. It is only through being honest that one is given the clues or wisdom on how to get to those places where the wonder and magnificence of total communion with the Great Mystery and Oneness are achieved.

Weighs the Truth, the Clan Mother of the Third Moon Cycle, is the Keeper of Solutions who only shares her wisdom with those who are willing to accept the truths of their paths. The ones who are willing to honestly question their actions and thoughts have shown that they possess hearts that are pure enough to receive the life-changing visions that lead to wholeness.

ACCEPTANCE
✖

Acceptance is the road to a quiet mind. When one can accept the truth of a situation, then the clear understanding of what the next step should be comes without confusion. When human beings understand that the past cannot be changed, they have gathered one form of acceptance. When these same people come to a place of feeling acceptance, there is no room for denial. Without denial, we are free to respond to the growth opportunities that may have originally been hidden from us by the critical voices of the past. There is only one place where true acceptance is found, and that place is in the present moment of the Now.

Indian children were once taught by their Elders to be in a constant state of alertness and were trained to observe everything in their surroundings. Being authentically aware of what was happening had its own rewards: game for dinner, early warning systems, lessons on the animals, prevention of accidents, and acceptance of any situation that needed an instant, independent solution.

Since the advent of modern conveniences and more leisure time, human beings have turned more to being dissatisfied with life, denying how things change, and lacking acceptance of the truth. Weighs the Truth, the Clan Mother of the Third Moon Cycle, teaches us how to let go of the past and how to face the future with confidence and conviction. These lessons are learned through the destruction of denial through acceptance, and through adopting dependability—toward self and others—as a way of being.

FEATHERS

><

My Elders taught me that feathers represent lofty ideals and the grace of inspiration that is based in truth. The straight quill of the feather shows us that the path of truth is constant and does not deviate.

Inside any seeker of truth there is a longing for spiritual awakening. In the Native American culture, we are taught that the Spirits ride the wind. Wind, found in humans, is called the breath. When we breathe air into our bodies we are able to access the creative inspiration we need. Allowing Spirit to use the breath, to enter our physical forms, is illuminating. That same Spirit is a part of the wind that lifts the wings of Eagle, soaring high. Of all the Earth Mother's creatures, eagles fly closest to the light of Grandfather Sun, illuminating lofty ideals and purity of purpose.

If you long for the extraordinary experiences of life, it may be time to breathe more. Allow the aliveness of Spirit to access your body. You may be surprised when you become inspired for flight.

HONOR
⋈

According to Native American concepts, the verb *to honor* means to show respect for the Sacred Space, the Sacred Point of View, and the possessions of another. To honor the deeds of another is to show our appreciation for that person's contributions to a community, family, or individual. To bring honor to our family, Tribe, Clan, or to our country is to give of ourselves above and beyond what is normally expected of any group member.

To honor the Self is a balancing act that can take much practice. In American Indian culture, the word *sacrifice* originally meant "to make sacred." If we honor ourselves, our roles, our abilities and our talents, we must see these things as sacred. When we choose to share those sacred gifts with others, we can honor ourselves and those we serve only if we do so without looking for reward, accomplishing each deed with a happy heart. Our reward is the joy we finding in giving to those we *choose* to serve.

Is it time to adopt the attitude of a happy heart when you accomplish your daily tasks? If you choose to, the happy heart brings honor to every act you perform.

SACRED WARRIOR'S VOW
✖

The vow of every warrior
Who ever rode the plains
To protect the children
Forever will remain.
Those hearts full of courage
Promised to defend
The Elders and Life Givers,
Until the bitter end.
Those times are a memory,
To many, a bygone day,
But a new Sun is dawning
Upon the Warrior's Way.
The peaceful Warriors awaken,
Their hearts hear the cry,
Their eyes embrace the vision,
Found in Brother Eagle's eye.
They rise from every Nation,
Ready to claim the right,
To stand as men of courage,
The defenders of the light.

DEPENDABILITY

Respect is often earned through one's dependability. If others know that a person can be relied upon to speak honestly, to act in times of crisis, to contribute with generosity, to use wisdom in making decisions, and to be faithful to family and friends—that person has earned respect.

In ancient times, Indian people demanded a high level of integrity from anyone within the Tribe who was to have a place of leadership. The men or women who were to hold a place of honor in adulthood had to earn the respect of their Tribe starting at puberty and continue to be dependable their whole lives. Erratic behavior, laziness, disrespect for Elders, or criticism of others could mark a person as lacking leadership ability.

The way people lived their lives was the manner in which they earned the right to be depended upon. Every Tribe depended upon their leaders and the decisions those leaders made for the survival of the whole.

In modern times, in all cultures, we often forget to consider our children, our mates, and our Elders. These members of our families would like to depend upon us. When we examine our lives, we must ask ourselves if we have earned their trust. The past cannot be changed. But in the present, we have the opportunity to make amends by changing our attitudes and actions, remembering how it felt when we were not supported. There is no need to pass that hurt to the next generation.

REASON

OUR REASON WILL NEVER DECIPHER
THAT WHICH OUR HEARTS CANNOT
UNDERSTAND.

Using our gifts of intellect, reasoning ability, and deduction is not enough when we are observing the Mystery of Life. There are many things happening in our world that may seem like miracles to those who have not experienced them. When we experience the wonders of life firsthand, we feel it to the core of our beings. These personal experiences may defy rational explanation. It is certain, however, that when we walk through that experience we know and feel our certainty because our hearts understand. No one can ever take that away from us.

Is it time to review how your head may have controlled your heart, creating self-doubt instead of certainty?

DIVINE JUSTICE

⚎

Justice can teach the wounded,
Who lash out in their pain,
How it feels to be the recipient
Of another person's blame.
Justice can show the swing of
The scales that weigh the truth,
Measuring the wisdom of Elders
Against the follies of youth.
Justice pledges to oversee
The Creator's equal care
For every part of Creation,
Teaching us how to share.
Within Divine justice,
Freewill was given to all;
Our choices carry the burden
Of our judgment calls.
One day, we'll stand in the truth
Of Great Mystery's light,
Where we will weigh the balance
Of our personal wrongs and rights.

VALUE OF THE SPIRITUAL ESSENCE

Human beings cannot understand another's life until they have carried the weight of that person's burdens, listened to that person's words, felt that person's pain, observed that person's actions, and walked along that person's path, sharing the other's greatest longings and aspirations. Understanding these things, we must then be able to sleep at that person's fire, sharing every part of the other human being's dreams and nightmares.

Only then can we see beyond the exterior and only then are we free to understand our common humanness. From this vantage point, we may see beyond the tangible frailties and into the Spiritual Essence called the Orenda, finding the Eternal Flame of Love.

The Ancestors say that when we judge others for their faults, we have lost our balance and our personal connection to the Maker. When we are critical, holding others in contempt, we are actually demonstrating our personal fear that the Creator may be judging the crooked trail we are following. "Playing God" does not suit humankind. Is it time for you to drop any holier-than-thou attitudes?

GOOD MEDICINE AND DIVINE LAW
❌

NATIVE AMERICAN MEDICINE AND SACRED
TRADITIONS NEVER DEPEND UPON WRITTEN LAWS,
BUT UPON THE PERSONAL QUALITIES AND SENSE OF
INTEGRITY DEMONSTRATED BY THE GIFTED.

Throughout time, gifted people have been called to share their wisdom and their commitment by serving others. In the course of history, many have used their natural abilities to support the growth of their Clans and Tribes. The Traditions that have been passed down to the following generations have flourished under the watchful eyes of faithful servants of the Earth Mother and the Creator.

Written laws about how the Medicine was to be used have not existed. Oral messages about how stories were to be told and how Traditions were to be followed have supplied the guidelines. Every Tribe has depended upon the integrity of the gifted, insuring that the ministrations received were correct and healing. The abuse of natural abilities has occurred from time to time. The harm created is not punished by written laws. The resulting harsh life lessons, which bring the abuser's misuse of Good Medicine back into balance, are the sole property of the Creator.

This kind of justice may seem strange to other races. This balancing of incorrect use of integrity may not be swift, but it does happen. This way of justice provides any abuser of Sacred Trust with the lessons personally needed to correct the behavior.

Weighs the Truth, the Clan Mother of the Third Moon Cycle, reminds us that all people will reap the harvest of the seeds they have sown. Impeccable integrity, when one is placed in a role of trust, is weighed on a moment-to-moment basis. Is your integrity in need of review, so that the seeds you have sown will return the kind of harvest you want to receive?

SPLITTING THE BLANKET
✄

The Traditions surrounding marriage in matrilineal Tribes is certainly an eye-opener for most non-Native people. From long ago until present time, only women own property among the Iroquois Nations.

Long ago, if the Iroquois men wanted to go to war, they had to get permission from the Clan Mothers. This made sense because the burden of losing the men in battle would then fall to the women who would have to raise their families alone. Every material thing from a marriage belonged to the wife and when she felt the marriage was not working, she was the one to split the marriage blanket by placing the husband's clothes, his half of the marriage blanket, and his hunting items outside the longhouse. He would then have to go back to his mother's Clan in shame to live with them in their longhouse, bearing the common knowledge that he had not been a good husband, provider, or father.

Although the decision to split the blanket and end a marriage was not taken lightly, the burden of a just decision rested with the woman. The man was also free to leave if the wife was not fulfilling her duties, but he had to leave without anything but his personal possessions.

Imagine the effect this custom would have on our modern world. Could this practice insure that both marriage partners would strive to get along? Could an arrangement of this kind ensure that both parties would take their roles of union and devotion as sacred, weighing the truth of their love for one another against the consequences of improper behavior?

WEIGHS THE TRUTH
✂

The Protectress of the meek
Weighs the truth for all to see,
Divine Law, seeking balance,
Setting the spirit free.

And here amid the chaos
Of earthly trials she stands,
Ready to issue justice,
Compassion in her hands.

She answers when deception
Shows the destructive face
Of human greed and hatred,
Dividing every creed and race.

Keeper of Great Mystery's laws,
Whose guiding ways we seek,
May we accept the Oneness of
The truths we hear you speak.

Weighs the Truth, the Clan Mother of the Third Moon Cycle, asks us to notice the burdens of bigotry that we carry and the sorrows that we keep when we judge others for any reason. This Clan Mother shows us a way to balance the unjustly weighted scales of our own unfairness by finding something we can admire about anything we have formerly judged as being "less than." Little may we know that our criticism of others has bled into our treatment of ourselves. The parts of ourselves that are ashamed of not being perfect are the same parts that have to live with our mental computations, judging the lack of worth in others. We can only arrive at the justice found in Divine Law when we break the pattern of seeing life through the unequal eyes of criticism.

RIGID AND ABSOLUTE
✂

ONE OF THE MOST DANGEROUS
HUMAN CREATIONS IS A RIGID
AND ABSOLUTE CODE OF ETHICS
THAT DISALLOWS FREEWILL AND
THE NATURAL DEVELOPMENT
OF INTUITIVE INTEGRITY.

The rebellion of the human spirit against other-determined laws or codes that wield punishment, without exception or compassion, have brought countless civilizations and religions to their knees.

The intuitive integrity that evolves through personal experience and freewill allows humankind to make and to correct mistakes in judgment and behavior. The unseen Code of Ethics that urges humanity to evolve is quite simple. Everything that we do to another is eventually experienced inside ourselves because "the grand illusion" is separation.

Could it be time for you to use your freewill by making a personal creed you choose to live by?

DAY OF RECKONING
⋇

A day of reckoning lies across the path of every human being who walks the Red Road of physical life. Our ability to respond to the effects created through our actions, thoughts, and words is dependent upon the individual's sense of integrity and personal accountability. We develop our willingness to be reckoned with through the clarity of our personal intent, coupled with the content of our deeds. The sincere desire to deal fairly with others, to admit our shortcomings, and to make amends where needed is the mark of a person worthy of trust.

It is evident when people have made peace with themselves, with others, and with the Great Mystery. The individuals who have found this type of inner peace have no need to defend the past or the present life they lead. These serene spirits have no fear of a day of reckoning because they have already weighed and balanced the truth, reckoning and healing the results for themselves.

Weighs the Truth, the Clan Mother of the Second Moon Cycle, reminds us: There is no other time that better suits the self-reckoning, healing process than Now. Is it time for you to look at healing any fear of being reckoned with or called on your behavior by another? If you look at places you would like to improve your reactions or responses to life, changing them for yourself, the needed inner serenity will follow.

HUMAN HUNGER
✄

The voices of the homeless
Cry out in their pain,
Asking for a crust of bread
Or shelter from the rain.
Abandoned Elders and children,
Forgotten by the score,
Cry silent tears of loneliness,
Drowned by the city's roar.
War-torn nations bathed in blood
Forget the innocents' plight,
Yet, there they lay dying,
Not caring who was right.
The sick and weary travelers
Of the world seek some rest,
A solace for the hungry heart,
The common human quest.
Some hearts hunger for the love
That they have never known.
Some hearts ache with longing,
To fly where Eagle has flown.
Greedy hearts seek power,
Others look for ways to share,
Earth Mother loves without judgment,
And shows us how to care.

THE FALLACY OF DOMINATION
✖

The abuse of power, as seen in the need to control the masses, has been fueled by greed throughout time. The fallacy of dominant societies is found in the historical evidence that there will always be another power-hungry opposition that will come along to play the role of conquerors.

The greedy power brokers of the world have not realized that it is impossible to dominate the human spirit. Trying to permanently break the spirit of any race or group of human beings is futile. A temporary conquest can be achieved, but the human spirit will always rise again. In the following generations, the changes found in *the will* are imbued with more determination and a deeper understanding of the roles life offers.

Some people say that the Sacred Hoop of Life was broken when Native Americans lost their lands and freedom. My Elders have taught me that this Circle of Life, the Sacred Traditions that represent our Medicine Wheel, has not been broken. The Faithful, the Wise Ones, have kept the fires burning, ensuring that the goodness, the strength of spirit, and the Beauty Way of our people will always endure. Our task is rediscovering the spirit and healing the fallacies that insist that any spirit can be dominated or broken forever.

Weighs the Truth, the Clan Mother of the Third Moon Cycle, asks us to see the overview of our lives and to notice where we have given our authority to glib lies that tell us we cannot rise again. We all have places inside of ourselves where we believe that we cannot succeed, heal, make a better life, or overcome a challenge. It is a lie. Have we given away our authority and desire to survive? Do you need to release a lie you believed, reclaiming your spirit's authority in order to grow?

THE RACCOON'S LESSONS
⚌

The forest was full of homeless and wounded creatures after the great fire. The Raccoon Tribe ravaged all the nearby mountain cabins and brought food to the hungry. The Tribe of little bandits worked long and hard hours to supply what was needed to help the other friends of the forest.

Mama Raccoon was busier than most of the others of her Tribe, mending the cuts and bandaging the burns of those who came for assistance. Days dragged into moons, and still the needy came in hordes. Mama Raccoon was the protectress of the frail, the children, the injured, and the underdog. She took her mission very seriously and labored day after day with little relief or rest. The other raccoons became increasingly worried because Mama was close to collapse.

One morning, Mama Raccoon fell over, barely alive. The others took her to the burrow and nursed her as best they could. In her lapses of dreams and consciousness, Mama Raccoon heard the Earth Mother saying, "You gave all of your strength to others, forgetting to weigh the consequences. The little bandit in you who robbed food from those who had a lot, giving it to those who had none, has lost her balance. In order to heal, you will need to see the error of robbing yourself of all your energy and giving it away, leaving you with none."

Mama Raccoon learned these lessons and got well. Now she teaches these same lessons to humankind, reminding them to give to the best of their abilities without robbing themselves of their health or sense of well-being.

THE WEIGHING OF POWER
⚏

Those who possess the power of knowing and trusting their Medicine grasp that power lightly. They understand that by clutching or holding on to the *idea* of power, one becomes possessed by it.

These wise individuals never need to defend who or what they are, because they are confident in the Medicine they carry. The precious understanding of one's role in life and one's gifts is between each individual and the Creator. The Earth Mother protects these gifted ones because they have come home to the Self, examining and working on all their weak points.

Through using the cold eye of self-examination, these individuals do not point fingers at others. They understand that there is no need to fight against jealousy or ignorant attempts to slander. They choose to maintain the dignity of their inner peace, and that is why we call them the Faithful and the Peacemakers.

WATCHING THE COMING OF SPRING
✖

The throes of winter, dying hard,
*   left snow in the shade of trees.*
Teasing, dipping, and dancing,
*   the sunlight warmed me briefly,*
*   then, like a fickle lover, disappeared.*
With raging winds or warming breeze,
*   will spring's sweet breath*
*   change the snow to rain?*
Can the thawing snows,
*   living in the mountain heights,*
*   send rushing waters to cleanse*
*   death's pale and frozen shade?*
Awaiting the return
*   of the Earth Blanket's green,*
I understood the reluctance of humans
*   to commit to one another.*
Fearing the cold,
*   they forgot how to love the snow.*

*Weighs the Truth, the Clan Mother of the Third Moon Cycle, asks us to rec-
ognize the signs of renewal in our lives and to be committed to the continuation of our growth. If we accept the truth of seasons changing, we must
accept the truth of the changes in people. When we grow in different directions from those we have loved, the old patterns die hard. The new will
bring many experiences that take us beyond our former comfort zones. The
old has to be cleansed before this renewal can blossom. Is it time to grow beyond your former limitations, cleansing the frozen places by loving them
equally? When you love all of life equally, renewal is at hand.*

WORSHIPING SELF-IMPORTANCE
✂

Those who seek to be glorified, adored, and set upon a pedestal have not yet discovered that it is ultimately a boring and lonely place. When one is no longer allowed to be human, fallible, and feeling, the end result is disaster. When the false self-image or godlike status is shattered, only emptiness and degradation are allowed to remain.

The real adepts of our world have chosen to remain humble, self-effacing, and beautifully human. They walk gently on the Earth Mother, embracing the love of simply being. Their desire to experience, and to show compassion, is the essence that fires and fuels their passion for life.

Weighs the Truth, the Clan Mother of the Third Moon Cycle, shows us how easily we can become products of our own self-importance. This crooked trail haunts human history. The pitfalls are many. One of the final lessons of human wholeness is found in how people learn to handle fame. Whether the recognition is large or small, the effects of fame can lead to false self-image. Has any drive for fame thwarted your ability to see yourself? Have you mentally held yourself above others? Have you put someone on a pedestal, disallowing the validity of your Sacred Point of View? Authentic humility and compassion can bring balance.

WEIGHING THE FORCE OF INTENT
✖

The young men were learning to hunt with their bows and arrows. The finest archer in the Tribe was teaching them the techniques that would bring food to the People. The old hunter told the boys about a strange guidance system that he counted as the secret to his success. He made his own arrows and crafted them with love. He then pricked his finger with his knife, putting one tiny drop of blood on each arrow while he silently placed his intent inside of his creations.

The boys looked curious. What was the intent the Old One placed in his magical arrows? They did not have to wait long before the hunter told them.

"I return thanks to the Great Mystery for the creatures who will bring food to my family. I ask that my arrows be guided, making a clean and painless kill. Finally, I place the drop of my blood on each arrow to represent the bond of red blood that I share with my Four-legged Brothers, and the Winged Ones, who offer their bodies as food so our People may live. I show my gratitude to the Creator for guiding my hands and these arrows before I ever place one in a bow. That is how I know how far to draw my bowstring back. My honorable intent gives my arrows a strength of their own. My bow is never drawn all the way back. Using too much force would destroy the sacred intent my arrows already carry."

CROW MEDICINE—DIVINE LAW
✖

FEED YOUR STRENGTHS AND YOU WILL FLOURISH.
SUPPORT YOUR TRIVIAL WEAKNESSES AND YOU
WILL LANGUISH, WHILE YOUR SHADOW
FLOURISHES AND BECOMES STRONG.

When we pick on ourselves, the shadowy sides of our natures are given strength. This misuse of our freewill allows the shadow side to feed on our usable life force, inviting disaster.

When we continue to express ourselves freely, using our strengths to direct our efforts, we find balance and essential wholeness. When we support what is most creative and positive within us, and refuse to give in to anything that weakens our resolve, we find new strengths available, flowing unaided into our beings.

This is Divine Law. What side of your nature have you been feeding?

SINGLETON, Earl C. "Red" — Passed away peacefully at the age of 90 on October 31, 2003 in Redwood City. Born in Sacramento and raised in Petaluma, Earl lived in San Mateo for over 50 years. Earl C. "Red" Singleton, 2003 is survived by his wife of 53 years, Maryon Singleton, daughter Judith Singleton of Fremont, son Stephen Singleton and Daphne of San Mateo. He was Santa Barbara, sister June Catey of partner, Christopher Teasley, both of Chico and his companion, Copenhagen of San Mateo, He was much loved by many nieces & nephews. Earl owned a business. Auto Home Supply, in San Mateo for many years. He also worked at Breuner's for 13 years. He served as a San Mateo Public Works Commissioner of the Board of free-elected member of the San Mateo city charter. He rewrote the San Mateo 1986-1994 and as an holders who helped to found the Brown Bag Food Program in San Mateo also second Harvest Food Bank. He had also been active with Boy Scout Troop 27, San Mateo Branch, 1 and Transfigura-SIRS Damian Church in San Mateo, tion Episcopal service celebrating Earl A memorial service will be held on Saturday, November 8 at 1:00pm at Transfigura-Singleton's life will be held on Saturday.

Elizabeth Dorothy Weisbecker —

AGUILA, Andrea A
AHLGREN, Joyce A
BACH, Victor
CAFFERATA, Dolore
DelMONTE, Pamela
EMOND, Joseph P.
GEE, Dana Tiffany
HO, Florence
HORGAN, John F.
KE, Brother Theoph
KEFFE, John H., Jr. "
MARSHALL, Bert
McCANN, Eileen D.
McEVOY, Colleen Ma
MIDDLETON, John Pa
NOVY, Helen Forster
PAULUKONIS, Felicia
REIDY, Katherine E.

s born March 24, 1932 in Eg
City, New Jersey, to C
becker, a carpenter, and D
becker, a self started

DOES THE SHADOW CARRY CLOUT?
✖

ROTTEN BEHAVIOR, LIKE ROT IN AN APPLE'S CORE,
SPREADS OUTWARD, DEVOURING EVERY PIECE
OF INNOCENCE, POSITIVE CREATIVITY,
AND KINDNESS IN ITS PATH.

When we look at whether or not the shadow has clout, the answer has to be yes. We give it clout. When people lose sight of their positive, honest intent, and opt to feed the shadow that stalks the crooked trail, they have much healing to do before they can come back to balance.

The shadow side of human nature contains many types of rotten behavior. Sometimes this rotten behavior is directed toward others; sometimes it is imploded, feeding on self-destruction. In all cases, the shadow is then allowed to experience every kind of joy that it robbed from the essential Self. This produces the feelings of helplessness and hopelessness in the person whose shadow is in control. Some feel helpless to stop hurting others. Others feel hopeless because they have rejected themselves through negative thoughts, giving the shadow the clout to devour their joy and self-esteem.

Weighs the Truth, the Clan Mother of the Third Moon Cycle, shows us that we can reclaim our wholeness. We must accept the truth within us, rejecting the lies the shadow wants us to believe. Through taking responsibility for our thoughts, we can heal the rotten behavior. The core-level healing comes from making peace with the shadow, instead of fearing it. Honor your clout, and the strength to heal will be yours once more.

INVOKING THE INFINITE
✂

Weighs the Truth watched as some of her human children gathered to conduct a Ceremony. The Circle was formed, and the spokesperson called out the sacred words to invoke the Great Mystery's assistance and presence. These human beings were learning one of her greatest lessons, self-determination. She had not asked them to return thanks, they had chosen to do the Ceremony, because their hearts were full.

All the people in the Circle took their turns by expressing their gratitude for the lessons they were learning. Little did they know that they were invoking the Infinite. An extension of Great Mystery's love walked among them, embodied with the eternal grace and inner peace that comes from taking on added responsibilities for the well-being of all life. As this Infinite Spirit touched their hearts, a change overtook their faces, lighting them from within. That beautiful balance of Spirit and human identity was reflected by the natural responses of each person in the Circle. Each person's individual self-determination to be of service fired every heart with passion.

Weighs the Truth was happy. She saw that these human beings had balanced the shadow side of ego with the determination of Spirit, coming to the place where they embodied the balance. They were becoming responsible Guardians—the infinite extensions of the Great Mystery's loving creation.

ACCEPTANCE OF THE WHOLE SELF

><

The balance and acceptance
Of all parts of the whole,
Come when we can honor
The lessons in every role.
The shadow reflects the lessons
Of every denial we hold.
The mind can thwart or assist,
Choosing to encourage or scold.
The body reacts to all thoughts,
Whether they hinder or aid;
Freewill determines the outcome,
As we choose to love or degrade.
The spirit watches in silence,
Nurturing the Eternal Flame,
Counting the losses and victories,
Of the "Will Versus Shadow Game."
The playing field of Mother Earth,
With the worlds of spirit unseen,
Affords a multitude of choices,
Lessons for every human being.
Wholeness to each is different,
Finding balance without denying,
That peace comes from acceptance,
From truth instead of from lying.

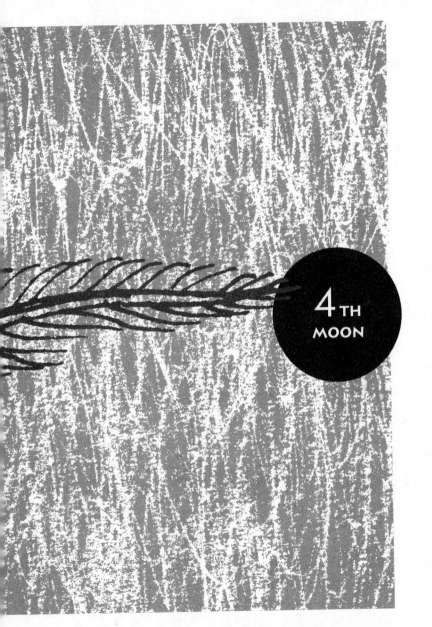

4TH
MOON

VISIONS, FEELINGS, AND THOUGHTS ARE ALIVE

Native Americans know that everything in life has spirit. All that we see in the tangible world is alive. Those things we cannot see as having form are just as alive as the solid forms of the natural world. Every thought has life force depending upon how much feeling it is connected to within the person. If the person envisions the thought, the mind's eye also adds life force to that idea by creating a picture or vision.

If the thought has deep emotion and imagination connected to it, there is a very good chance that the Dreamer or Visionary will be able to make that thought come to fruition. The secret is using the life force available to bring physical life to the dream or envisioned outcome.

In ancient times, our people had Dreamers who were very honored members of the Tribe because of their abilities of seeing. The Dreamers could access the needs of their Tribe and envision the successful outcome of the hunt, harvest, or journey.

The Clan Mother who is the Guardian of the Dreamers, Seers, and Oracles is Looks Far Woman. She is the Clan Mother of the Fourth Moon Cycle and teaches us how to properly use the aliveness of all our thoughts for positive ends. The awareness that our thoughts and emotions carry life force and do create results is not enough. We must be accountable for our internal thoughts and feelings—as well as for our outward physical actions.

SEEING THE SPIRIT
✄

Spirit breathes the aliveness
Into every flower and tree,
And fosters our connections
To life's Sacred Mystery.
The net that binds us together,
Is the spirit we hold in kind,
The abundant, unlimited expression
Of the Creator's breath divine.
Humankind is always looking
For ways to measure the soul,
Never really seeing the Spirit
That makes Creation a whole.
Fragments rest in every part
Of the natural world we know,
But when we forget the Oneness,
We fail to honor Creation's flow.
Spirit flows in unity through
The Source from which all came,
Visible to every seeker who
Has found the Eternal Flame.
That fiery connection to all life
Rests in the love that lies within,
A Oneness that gives us no recourse,
But to see the spirit in all our kin.

SEEING THE TRUTH OF CREATION
✂

The Wise Grandmother visited many other Clans and Tribes, sharing her wisdom. The Clans that lay in the west surprised her when she heard their prayers in the Purification Lodge. Some were beginning their prayers by telling the Maker of All Life how pitiful and poor they were. The Medicine Woman knew better than to point a finger or make these people wrong for the misunderstandings they carried, so she silently waited until it was time to share her prayer, and then she spoke a prayer of gratitude.

"Great and Eternal Mystery of Life, Creator of All Things, I give thanks for the beauty You put in every single one of Your creations. I am grateful that You did not fail in making every stone, plant, creature, and human being a perfect and whole part of the Sacred Hoop. I am grateful that You have allowed me to see the strength and beauty of All My Relations. My humble request is that all of the Children of Earth will learn to see the same perfection in themselves. May none of Your human children doubt or question Your wisdom, grace, and sense of wholeness in giving all of Creation a right to be living extensions of Your perfect love."

Many heard the Wise Woman's words that twilight during the steam and songs of the Lodge. They began to walk taller after that and with a new inner dignity. They decided to show their gratitude for the beautiful part of the Creator's love that was placed inside of them, refusing to dishonor the Maker of All Life ever again.

SACRED POINT OF VIEW
✖

Every living thing and every human being has a Sacred Point of View. To deny any person, creature, plant, or stone its right to observe life from its personal vantage point is a misuse of authority. All life forms have a right to see the truth from their own experience and perspective. How these viewpoints meet and connect, meld and intertwine, creates the weaving of our common understandings of the tangible world.

Due to the varied Sacred Points of View of all life forms, the tangible world contains uncountable worlds within it. For human beings to begin to understand these worlds within worlds, we must learn to assume the different viewpoints of every living thing. Our dreams can allow us to see through the eyes of Jaguar or Eagle. We can become the rushing waters or dance with the lightning bolts in the stormy sky. The Dreamtime world is the place where the fabric of tangible and intangible meld, creating forms of pure energy. This world is the home of the Little People that children call fairies.

Could it be time for us to let go of our human arrogance and accept the wonder of seeing the billions of truths that are present within the Great Mystery's Creation? If we let go, maybe we will encounter the miracles of childhood we believed were only fantasies.

DREAMING THE WORLD

I have been the sunlight
On the open plain,
I have seen the wonders
Of earth drinking rain.
I have tasted the nectar
Of flowers and of dew,
I have been the hummingbird
Seeding love where I flew.
I have flowed with rivers,
Learning the water's songs,
Singing to every canyon,
As the river moved along.
All these dreams have lifted me
Beyond the worlds I knew,
Where I have lived the harmony
Of other Sacred Points of View.

DISCERNMENT
✖

Discernment is a part of seeing the truth in all things. To observe the obvious can take many years of training. In ancient times, Indian children were taught to sit silently and look at everything around them, noting every tiny detail. As adults, Native Americans could discern whether to trust others or not through observing these people's actions, their mannerisms, their treatment of their families, their willingness to work, and their words regarding others.

In the modern world, we often take people at their word because they talk as if they are honest, caring, or willing to take action. Their actions may not match up to their words, and because we have not been taught to observe for long periods of time, our discernment is lacking. Trust has to be *earned*. Due to families not being as strong as they once were, some people are lonely, making them easy prey.

We must watch, look, and listen before following anyone onto the frozen lake; then we have no need to worry about falling through the thin ice. The broken hearts and shattered trust created by lack of discernment can make us numb to the joy life offers. If we observe the obvious, honoring our feelings as internal warning signals, we can learn to trust our perceptions. The trust we gain in our discernment abilities is self-trust, Within the safety of self-trust we no longer need the old lessons of being led astray.

If you have been led astray, it may be time to develop self-trust, observing before you act.

OPENINGS OF THE ORENDA
✖

The little girl asked her wise Grandfather why the Great Mystery gave eyes to the Two-legged Tribe of humans. Grandfather smiled silently, remembering her Grandmother's eyes that were reflected in the Little One's face, then he replied.

"Your eyes can see the world around you and take in the beauty of Creation. Your eyes can shed the tears that cleanse your hurts, allowing you to heal. Your eyes were meant for seeing all that Yeodaze, the Earth Mother, places in your path so these things can be recorded as the memories of your passage in this Earthwalk. Yes, Little One, our eyes have many ways to teach us how to see truth.

"Your eyes can betray your thoughts and feelings to others because they are the openings to the Orenda, the Spiritual Essence. One day you will find a warrior to share your life with. When that time comes, you will be able to look into his eyes and see him with your heart. Through his eyes, the openings of his Orenda, you will know if his spirit can shelter you and if his heart is pure. When you look into his eyes, seek the truth of his nature.

If he looks away, he is not strong enough to shelter your love for him. If he looks directly into your eyes and allows your hearts to connect, adding his strength to your own, you will know that he is a courageous man worthy of sharing your Earthwalk."

OMENS
✖

Omens signal that Great Mystery
Is offering us a clue;
If we pay attention,
We may count our victory coup.
If we ignore the feelings,
Knowing that comes from within,
Failing to follow that wisdom,
We've denied the feminine.
There's a magic deep inside us
That comes from an open heart;
Sister Raven comes flying,
To show us intuition's art.
If we grasp the message,
And if we make it our own,
The doors of mystery fly open
To welcome each seeker home.

If the answers you seek are hard to find, try asking nature to bring you a signal. Then use all of your senses—pay close attention!

THE GIFT OF PROPHECY
✖

The twin brother and sister had passed many winters, earning places of respect as Wise Ones of their Tribe. Their minds had always been connected and were attuned to each other, as well as to the Spirit World. The old man was blessed with the gift of seeing events, and his sister's gift was in feeling and sensing the vision's meaning.

One day a wanderer came to their camp, having heard of their powers of prophecy. He had many questions and a curious mind. He asked the Old Ones how they knew they had the gift of prophecy, and the Wise Woman replied.

"The gift is something that comes unbidden. It consumes you with pictures and feelings that do not reflect the present moment. It takes great discipline on the Seer's part to stand rooted in both worlds. It is the responsibility of the gifted one to see the truth, and relay that truth without taking another's will away. Misusing the gift to gain power and control, or to hurt another, assures that the gift will be taken away."

The Wise Man continued his sister's thought by saying, "When one can feel another's intention, and see the events on that person's path with clarity, it often brings sadness. The Seer knows that the lessons of life must be learned through experience. The sorrow of seeing another's future anguish is often a burden. Prophecy teaches us that we cannot change another's path; they must do that themselves. We must see and speak the truth, and then we must be willing to offer comfort and compassion to all people trying to find their way."

SPIRITS

SPIRITS ARE NOT MEAN! PEOPLE ARE MEAN!

—PABLO QUINTANA
COCHITI PUEBLO

Looks Far Woman teaches us about the gifts of talking to Spirit and the gifts of prophecy. This Clan Mother of the Fourth Moon Cycle is the wise and gentle teacher who knows that we humans are the only ones who direct meanness at one another. We are the directors of energy who use and misuse the ideas of love and fear.

It is through our human jealousy and envy that our thoughts take form and are directed negatively toward others. Thoughts and feelings are alive and can enter the awareness of others. The Spirits of Nature have no jealousy, or envy, or hidden agendas. It is only the unhealed emotions and intents of human beings—still hanging in time and space—that wreak havoc in the lives of others. Even these misdirected emotions cannot harm others if they have laughter in their hearts and smiles on their faces.

ADORATION

Adoration can blind us
To the deceiving ways of pain,
To users who pretend friendship,
But are seeking material gain.
Adoration can confuse us
Into giving away our hearts.
Instead of sharing the deep love,
That heartfelt caring can impart.
Adoration tends a rocky field,
Where nothing seems to grow,
But sees a phantom field of dreams,
Forgetting to seed, water, and hoe.

Adoration's harvest comes with frost,
The biting winter of broken dreams,
Having placed another, at all costs,
Above the wisdom of earned esteem.

If you have adored another person, putting him or her on a pedestal, without allowing him or her to earn your esteem, it may be time to take back some of that blind faith. Could it be that you have seen your best qualities projected outside of yourself so you won't have to own who you are?

DREAMING OUR WHOLENESS
✄

At times, the Human Tribe will have recurring dreams about the lessons we need to learn in order to achieve wholeness within the Self. These dreams can come over a period of years or on a more regular basis. Oftentimes we will dream about someone visiting us to give a message over and over again. Sometimes that dream person is of the opposite sex and can represent the other side of our nature, since every person has a male and a female side. This kind of dream can portend that we are making progress in developing both sides of our nature, coming into balance with our potential and our wholeness.

Looks Far Woman, the Clan Mother of the Fourth Moon Cycle, teaches us that dreams are important. Our dreams can represent a hidden part of our consciousness, ways to work out problems, warnings of the pitfalls of certain behavior patterns, omens, future possibilities, and a host of other things that we seem to be too busy to notice during our waking hours.

The symbols in our dreams are usually interpreted by the culture we grow up in. These symbols can tell us many things about ourselves and are simple to understand if we have an idea of what they mean. When we dream of a visitor of the other gender who brings a message, Divine Union is at hand. Every man will reach wholeness through developing his female side and balancing it with his maleness. Every woman reaches her potential by developing her male side and balancing it with her femaleness. We are asked to look at the other sides of our natures with compassion. Any person who blames the other sex for anything is refusing to heal that opposite side of themselves.

SEEING THE DREAM
✖

The Spirits visited the Grandmother who slept in the wigwam, bringing her a vision of her grandson's future mate. The child had passed eight winters and was still with his mother. He would pass many more winters before he met the woman who would bear his children, but the Grandmother knew that she was being given the sign that it was time for her to start making the ceremonial buckskins that the couple would wear on their wedding day.

Over the seasons that passed, Grandmother gathered all the special materials she would need to make the wedding regalia. She worked many moons on each garment over the years. When the grandson found the love of his life, the young man's mother smiled to herself. The young woman was the one Grandmother described from the dream of long ago.

When the Sun came that marked the day of union, the proud couple stood before the fire in the regalia Grandmother had made them. They jumped the fire together, symbolizing the bond between them, merging their union with the Eternal Flame of Love. Grandmother's dream was fulfilled. The promise of love had come to fruition.

Even though her earthly form had gone into the Other Side Camp many seasons before, the truth in her dreams allowed Grandmother to leave her grandson a legacy. The legacy was the realized dream of her love.

DREAMING THE MATE

Dreamwalker comes softly,
　　Bringing visions of delight,
　　　　Where in dreams he visited
　　　　My slumber last night.

My heart is in your pocket,
　　So tenderly refrain
　　　　From pressing on it,
　　　　Lest it should break
　　　　　Before we meet again.

Dreamwalker come hold me
　　Against your breast tonight,
　　　　So I may know the ecstasy
　　　　Of two hearts burning bright.

And you will know my spirit
　　Has visited you once more,
　　　　With devotion as resounding
　　　　As waves, crashing to the shore.

LOOKS FAR WOMAN

Mother, teach me how to see
The shining light of stars,
The faces of the Ancestors,
In worlds both near and far.

Show me how to welcome
The visions appearing to me,
Seeing the truth in detail,
Unraveling each mystery.

Walk me through the Dreamtime
Of altered time and space,
That I may share these visions
With every creed and race.

Doorkeeper of all dimensions,
I seek your Medicine Ways
Of how to earth my visions,
Seeing truth, inside me, today.

Looks Far Woman, the Clan Mother of the Fourth Moon Cycle, reminds us that we are in the ever-present moment of eternal Creation. We have the ability to see past, future, and all probabilities when we are fully present. What does it mean to be fully present? It means to have no attention or thought on how it will be in future. It means freeing ourselves of regret or lament about our past. It means ridding ourselves of the need to control any outcome of what we create in the moment. It means seeing ourselves clearly without masking our personal intent. It ultimately means having no chatter in our mental process and being attentive to what is happening in the moment. Being present takes practice and is a sure route to seeing the truth in every moment of your life.

AT WHAT COSTS?

What senses and perceptions have we neutered or suppressed through the false sophistication we use to hide our common human frailties?

The wise person knows that those healed senses can bring renewal, making us aware of the multitude of worlds that surround us. This simple understanding stands at the core of human potential, holding the open door that invites us to drop our masks. Without the blinders, we may remember who we really are and the powers of perception we hold. At the very least, we could be fortunate enough to rehabilitate our human compassion and sensitivity.

A FINAL TEST OF DREAMING
✖

The ultimate initiation of a visionary or dreamer comes when that individual dreams of abundance for everyone. This selflessness is not an act of conscience, but rather an act of wisdom, forged from experience. If humans exist on our planet whose most basic needs are not being met, while others have more than they will ever need, something is drastically wrong.

Any dream that does not include everyone is a vision created from limited perception, or in some cases, greed. The training regime of the Southern Seers who were my teachers is emphatic in this regard. If everyone is not considered worthy of having plenty, the Circle of Life is not being honored. If dreamers cannot see the unbroken family circle created by all life forms, they have not grown into their potentials nor ever really experienced the reality of Oneness.

When is the last time you remembered to include the needs of every single human in your prayers or in your vision of what the future should become?

IRIDESCENT REALITY

The pristine edges of reflection
That border the intuitive mind,
Refract the prisms and concepts,
Multiple mirrors of humankind.

Somewhere in the house of mirrors,
The mystery begins to unfold.
The blending of every nuance
Bringing the Oneness to behold.

Iridescent reality blends
Every shining moment in time,
Every awakening revelation,
That marks humanity's climb.

Spiraling onward—
  Beyond the place
    We have named "The Void of the Unknown."
Embracing the newness,
  In spite of our fears,
    Is the Good Medicine we've learned to own.

INTERNAL REVELATION

The predawn darkness reflected the last silver light of the waning moon. She watched the ghostly shapes of the naked chokecherry trees as they seemed to dance. With expectation and a little fear of waiting in the dark, she remembered that her Elders had told her that Grandfather Sun would return from his lodge after his rest, bringing the dawn.

She shivered while she waited, wanting desperately to give thanks for this precious day. She had come to understand many things in her young life, but it was very important for her to share her latest understanding by returning thanks.

The first rays of sunlight touched the sky, filling her with the warmth of expectation. She told Grandfather Sun how she had come to find the Totem who had pledged to be her Spirit Helper. She cried as the gratitude for her new Creature-teacher silently spilled from her heart.

Suddenly, out of the center of the brilliant sunbeams, she saw the figure of her Totem's Spirit emerge, bathed in amber light. There was the Golden Eagle whose spirit had plucked something out of her eyes during the previous night's healing ceremony. Her eyes, crossed since birth, were now aligned, giving her perfect vision. The illuminating healing had given her more than clear vision; because of her internal revelation that she was a sister to Eagle, her heart could clearly see with love.

DELUSIONS

The delusions that humankind buys into are astounding. It seems that we are bound to our limited perceptions of life, based upon the belief systems that we have encountered along our individual paths. It frightens most human beings to think that the tangible reality could melt, giving new awareness of other worlds that exist in the same time/space as the physical world.

Going beyond the *seen* and the *solid* has its own rewards. My Mayan/Yaqui/Aztec teacher Joaquin Muriel Espinosa taught me two ways that humans usually create their personal delusions:

> By denying or doubting their own perceptions.

> Faulty perceptions that come through the accidents of untrained senses.

BLINDED BY ABSOLUTE AUTHORITY

The organizations and groups that have tried to set themselves up as the absolute authorities in any culture have tried to blind the masses. These organizations have used absolute authority to twist the truths of any who spoke out, trying to discredit any opposition. They have used guilt to rule the opinions of the undecided, creating hypocrisy and fear. The resulting witch-hunts were used to prove that their way was the only true way. The desire to destroy or slander anyone who was not a part of their belief system, religion, philosophy, or Tradition has created mass separation.

The mark of any group that uses this kind of despotism is their use of scapegoats to cover their true intentions to set themselves up as the ultimate authority. The desire to be the only *real* authority on anything, is a tragic misuse of power, being based on selfish drives and having no desire to serve humanity as a whole.

We need to be grateful for the truths that this type of behavior allows us to see. We clearly see the truth of absolute authority's futility, trying to destroy that which cannot be destroyed—the personal inner knowing of each individual's honest connection to the Great Mystery. That sacred connection, and the inner knowing it creates, cannot be controlled by misplaced guilt, lies, or pack mentality.

LOSING SIGHT OF THE PATH
✄

The Clan Mother grieved the wandering ways of her human children. Looks Far Woman knew that her own lessons, in allowing her children to see for themselves, were a part of her growth. It was so difficult to see the Human Tribe hurting themselves. Their all-too-human lessons were painful to bear when she saw the anguish that was created through the hard knocks they continually experienced.

Her mind's eye flashed with the pictures of the sidetracks they took. Some wandered away from the sacredness of life through their woundedness, broken hearts, and lost dreams. Others followed the empty paths of greed for money, fame, or power, which promised glittering, superficial values. In truth, those who had been seduced by greed just needed the affirming recognition that they were loved.

These pain-filled children were unaware of their broken connections, to the Self and to the Maker, that had created the short circuits that caused them to lose sight of the path. Some sold out, others were betrayed by their inabilities to heal their own pain, but all of her wandering children had lost the insight that could point the way home.

Looks Far Woman stood between worlds, at the Golden Door of Illumination, finally realizing that she had some lessons of her own. She could learn many things while holding the door to illumination open for others. Reminding herself of this, she discovered that her lesson in this situation was to learn *patience!*

OBVIOUS STUPIDITY
✕

When the truth is sitting
Right in front of our noses,
We are asked the question,
Of what the truth exposes!
Were we afraid to look?
It wasn't hard to see.
Were we afraid of change?
The truth holds the key.
Let's blame it on Coyote!
He tricked us again!
All the time pretending
That he was our friend!
Say, "Ouch," to the lesson,
Then maybe we'll agree,
We can also see our lessons
Through obvious stupidity!

Sometimes the backdoor lessons are the best. What seems to be obvious stupidity, can also give us the abilities to laugh at ourselves. If the old saying is right, we should appreciate the laughter: The more seriously you take the game, the less chance you have of winning! *Is it time for you to lighten up and laugh at yourself? Forget that question; it's always time for us to see ourselves as Tricksters! After all, we tricked ourselves into becoming human beings, didn't we?*

OBSERVATION OF HUMAN NATURE
✖

THOSE WHO OBSERVE HUMAN NATURE SEE THAT
THOSE WHO OBSERVE NOTHING THINK THAT LIFE
HAPPENS *TO* THEM. WHAT HAPPENED TO THE
FREEWILL CHOICE OF DECIDING *TO BE?*

Those who hold the viewpoint that life happens to us, and is not of
our own making, forget that the Creator gave everyone freewill.
Some people say that they did not ask to be born, they did not ask
to have a rotten life, and they did not ask to have everything go
wrong.

This is an interesting idea—total and ultimate lack of responsibility. Denial of freewill, the lack of gratitude—setting up more
negative, victimlike experiences, and self-created blindness. The
inability to respond to life comes when we no longer feel the aliveness. We go numb when we deny any feeling that comes up during
our experiences, creating an unnatural barrier to self-expression.
When we can't feel, it is almost impossible to be a witness to the
Mystery of Life. How can we truthfully observe what we refuse to
feel?

SILENT VISION

The four-day Ceremony was over. The Holy People returned thanks for the powerful Medicine and visions that had been bestowed on the participants. Life-changing events had happened in front of the witnesses who had willingly stood as supports for the dancers. The air still crackled with the sacredness of Spirit, touching the lives of all the People.

Back in the lodge, Little Fox had quietly approached his father, wanting to know what his father had experienced in his vision. Having passed nine winters, his curiosity outweighed his sense of proper attitude and reverence. Gently, and with ultimate patience, the boy's father replied.

"Little Fox, there are some things so sacred that they may only be experienced wordlessly. When that sacredness happens in a person's life, the heart and the vision become as one. That silent vision of the heart is made a part of the person's spirit forever. To try to explain it to another would soil the sacredness, reducing the Medicine's strength to the frailty of mere human words."

BUILDING THE DREAM
✂

Truthspeaker sat with her niece in the cool afternoon breeze, mending moccasins. Little Beaver loved to be with her aunt because the younger woman always got truthful answers to her questions. Being a young mother, Little Beaver's questions multiplied as fast as her children grew.

"Auntie, I would like to make my dream for a larger lodge for my family come true, but something always comes up, taking away the materials we have gathered for another purpose."

Chuckling softly, Truthspeaker replied, "That is life's way, Little Beaver. The lesson is in learning to build your dreams the way your namesake builds her dam. To understand how to do that, you must observe everything Beaver does. The truth of your observations will show the way."

Two moons later, Little Beaver was back at her Auntie's lodge, grinning from ear to ear and talking incessantly. "I understand, Auntie; I did it! I watched Beaver and found out that I wasn't supposed to save our materials, gathering everything before we started. We used everything we had, building our new lodge one room at a time. I was frightened at first, but when we used up what we had, the new materials we needed were easily found. Beaver kept on adding to her dam, cutting new trees when she needed them. I saw how she taught me. I copied her and built my dream."

Seeing how to build our dreams, one step at a time, keeps us from being blinded by overwhelming and confusing visions. Is it time for you to see the truth in each step on your path by using the resources you have now?

UNLIMITED SIGHT
><

True sight is many-faceted,
Taking form in many ways,
Like mental image pictures,
The ideas our thoughts convey.

The mind's eye can embrace
The dreams of what will be,
The visions and aspirations,
Or the daydream's fantasy.

We can see with our eyes,
Or with a heart that can feel;
We can use our fingertips,
To see the body's need to heal.

We can use our spirits
To see other, intangible worlds,
And we can use our reason
To see how solutions can unfurl.

Some say seeing is believing,
But the true witness surely knows,
Through believing, we can see all facets
Of the worlds our imaginations can show.

MASKS OR MIRRORS
✂

The roles that all human beings are asked to play in the course of life can reflect our versatile natures. We become friends, parents, lovers, providers, teachers, messengers, students, and a host of other identities that round out our human skills. Through developing the skills required to fulfill these roles, we develop our potentials.

The masks that can inhibit our growth are also found in the roles we play. The teacher who degrades a very bright student because his intelligence threatens the instructor wears a jealousy or fear mask. The parent who shames a child for having an illness that costs too much time and money is wearing an insensitive mask of immature selfishness. The mate who, in front of anyone else, naggingly speaks of the other mate with contempt is wearing the mask of resentment and revenge.

All of these masks reflect what needs to be healed inside the person wearing them. The astute observer makes a note of the behavior and says nothing in the way of judgment. These masks can only be peeled off when the mask wearers ask for help, having created miserable consequences with their behaviors. Sometimes seeing the truth can be a burden, because the observer knows exactly what is creating the upset or imbalance. The wise observers look within themselves, deciding to heal any similar masks they may be wearing.

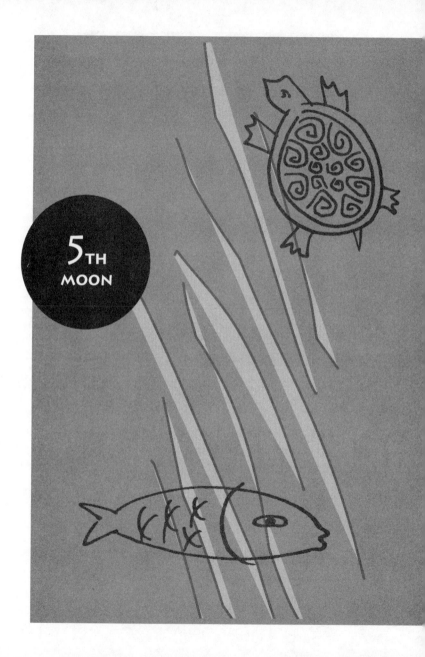

5TH
MOON

FIRST SOUNDS
⚏

The first sound every human being hears is the double heartbeat. In our mother's watery womb, we experience a sense of security and belonging because we hear our own heartbeats echoed by that of the mother who carries us for nine moons. When we are drawn into our Earthwalks through the miracle of birth, the second heartbeat disappears. Human beings know on a deep level that something is missing and many times go through life looking for the missing heartbeat.

The missing heartbeat is found when we listen to our Earth Mother and enter Tiyoweh, the Stillness. In that place of silence, we can hear the small, still voice within our hearts, and through that experience, we can rediscover our sense of security and belonging. The Earth Mother's heartbeat reminds us that we are never alone. Our true Mother, the Earth, is always present to nurture us and give us rest. All she asks is that we stop and listen for the second heartbeat.

Listening Woman, the Clan Mother of the Fifth Moon Cycle, teaches us that we can learn more by listening than by speaking. She teaches us that every living thing in nature speaks to us. Through the other life forms the Great Mystery placed upon the Earth, we find relationship, belonging, security, and wisdom. All living things can be our teachers if we learn to listen. Then we come to understand the Creator's purpose in sending human beings on the mission of searching for the second heartbeat—in finding that second heartbeat, we know that we are never alone.

TIYOWEH, THE STILLNESS
✖

When you learn to enter the Stillness and you sit
for hours without movement or sound, you may
hear the ONENESS.

From that understanding, you may discover the
sounds of the

ALL-UNFOLDING.

*Just make sure that the Divine Trickster has not fooled you into believing
that the gurgles in your bowels are the All, literally unfolding!*

LISTENING TO THE HEART
✖

Be like the mountain, reaching for the Sky Father—silent and watchful, majestic and still, enduring and reflective. Then, my child, you will know the inner fire of the Earth Mother. You will see that deep within her breast there is constant creation. This is one way Sacred Mountain shows Two-leggeds how to listen to the fire in their own hearts.

Listening Woman is the Keeper of Tiyoweh, the Stillness. This Clan Mother of the Fifth Moon Cycle teaches all of her human children how to Enter the Silence and how to feed their hungry hearts. The heart's food is passionate desire to create, to be, to understand, to love life, and to continue growth.

All of the answers to any questions that your heart seeks can be found in the Stillness. When you go there, you may encounter an echo. Do not be afraid; it is only the second heartbeat of our true Mother, the Earth. That second heartbeat signals that you have found your Sacred Path and returned home.

ALIVENESS

When we enter the Stillness and listen, we are given the opportunity to feel the aliveness that is around us. We give ourselves the opportunity to be a part of the vibrant, living, natural world. This place that we call Tiyoweh can open new understanding if we put the mind's voice aside. The Stillness brings a deep serenity into our hearts and vital life force into our bodies. When we practice Entering the Silence in nature, there is no frantic separation between the creatures of the forest and the gentleness in our hearts.

Taking the time to seek the silence of Tiyoweh, and to listen, is the act of a wise person. For it is in that place of serenity we become the Oneness. Through the Oneness, we discover the joyous truths of being alive.

If time is of the essence, taking the time to find and to listen to your essence may be very revealing. Are you at one with all that you can be? If not, you may need to take the time to be silent with yourself and honor the listening opportunity you can give to the Self.

LISTENING TO THE WHISPERS
✂

Listening to the whispers
That come through time and space,
The voices of the Ancestors
Of every creed and race.
Our silent spirits are waiting;
Inspiration is our desire.
The spark of understanding
Will set our hearts on fire.
Within that fiery vision,
The whispers call our names,
Asking those who listen
To carry the Eternal Flame.
The Flame is illumination
Of the love that lies within,
All creatures, Tribes, and Nations
Become family once again.
Are we really listening
To the whispers all around?
The voices within the circle
Are calling for common ground.
Where peace is the message,
Where no child stands alone,
And no hearts are broken,
Because we've all come home.

TALKING CIRCLES
✖

Whenever Native Americans come together in groups with things to discuss, there are certain rules that we always observe. Those unspoken rules show whether the participants were reared in a good way. No one has to make a comment about another person's behavior; it is evident through their actions. Listening is the foremost rule that determines a person's integrity and substance.

Talking Circles are what we use to bring problems out into the open, to find solutions, to share our feelings and experiences, and to honor the Sacred Points of View of every person present. To interrupt a speaker is to bring dishonor on his or her words, to bring dishonor on one's upbringing, one's family, Tribe, Clan, and Nation.

Among other cultures, this practice may seem alien because words are not considered part of the Sacred Breath of Life that holds a person's Sacred Point of View. When people are talking, they are not listening. When one person interrupts another, the lack of respect is apparent. When people are constantly talking about anything that comes to their minds, it is a sign that they have no self-reflective skills and do not feel the weight or sacredness that their words carry. If the words that are spoken carry no commitment or carelessly hurt another, the speaker is not in tune with Oneness. Anyone can claim to be spiritual. The truth of how far they have come on the Sacred Path is noted by simply seeing how they listen and how they speak.

MURMURS IN THE BREEZE

✂

When I walk the meadows,
Searching for rainbow's end,
The colors in the distance
Bring voices on the wind.
And there amid the flowers,
I listen without a sigh;
The spirits of the Ancients
Echo their hearts' reply.
Sacred murmurs on the breeze,
What would you say to me,
If I became the rainbow,
Or the standing tree?
Would you ask me to listen,
Or add my voice to yours?
Becoming a Guardian Spirit
Of these ancient woods.

If you can imagine, you can learn to understand the viewpoints of other life forms. Imagining how it feels to be another part of nature is a good exercise. It broadens our perspective and sometimes allows us to hear the viewpoints of our Relations in the natural world. Touching these living things through your feelings is always very healing.

LISTENING WITH OUR SENSES
✖

Two young women sat before the Grandmother. They had come to their Wise Elder to settle a dispute. The first young woman was quite a speaker, but she was nervous and could not look in her Elder's eyes. The other young woman was serene, but she had a problem speaking because of a speech defect.

The nervous girl kept twisting a lock of hair, babbling about why the Grandmother should decide in her favor, but she never told the Elder how the dispute had happened. The other girl simply answered the Old One's questions with short sentences that her mouth could form, looking into her Elder's eyes without shame.

The dispute was settled in the favor of the quiet young woman, and the Grandmother explained why. She told the girls that when she listened, she listened with all of her senses. These senses never failed her because they showed her the truth. She taught the girls that sometimes human beings need to listen to what people are *not* saying, rather than listening to their words.

MAGIC AND SWEET DREAMS

Crazy Raven comes cawing,
Flying through the night,
Looking for the children
Who need some delight.
These are the wounded children
Who have forgotten how to play,
Losing the magic of sweet dreams,
Having suffered along the way.
But Crazy Raven finds them,
His antics bring such cheer,
He flies through the Dreamtime,
Collecting all their tears.
If your life is full of sadness,
And nightmares mirror the flaws,
Listen—for Crazy Raven,
And answer his magical caw.
Rest again in sweet dreams,
Know that magic is here to stay,
A blessing from Earth Mother,
To the wounded,
*   who seek*
*   the Beauty Way.*

LISTENING TO THE WILL

Human beings are very adept at sabotaging the specific things that could make them happy. This art of subterfuge is usually a learned response. We are taught by modern society to take on the habits and patterns of those who were our role models, and usually these family members were taught not to listen to their feelings. *The will* is directed by our emotions and intuitive feelings. When we are cut off from these feelings, we enter a state of confusion. An example of this is lack of direction or a lack of the sense of wrong and right.

In Native culture, the Ancestors taught that listening to our feelings would give us a guideline. This lesson was in the context that the people of that day were deeply committed to the Creator, and to all living things. When the Ancestors felt something, they honored it. If taking an action did not feel right, it was not carried through.

Doing anything that would harm another living thing was a matter of conscience and will that could result in bringing harm back on one's Relations or the Self. Today, the Ancestor Spirits are teaching us how to listen to the will again. If we claim to be spiritual, we must take our own counsel, feel what it would be like to be on the receiving end of any action we take, and then make our decisions.

The ancient law of the Great Smoking Mirror still applies: *I am another one of yourself.* If we do anything harmful to another living thing or human being, we are ultimately doing it to ourselves.

HEARING THE PATTERN
✖

Water droplets course over the edge of the window, creating an uneven cadence as they drop to the boulders that line the hillside below the cabin. As it meanders across the Rio Grande river, a low, arrowlike cloud cuts my view of the emerald timberline. The fog moves in from the high peaks of the Rocky Mountains, telling me that the seasons are changing as I quietly monitor the movements of nature.

Today, the rain could change to snow. Inside the cabin, with the fire warding off the damp chill of morning, I relish the silence of the forest. Even with the rushing waters of the mighty river singing to me, I feel my awe of these majestic mountains and their watchful stillness.

Through my window, this glimpse of life's holiness becomes my teacher. The teacher speaks to me of the unimportance of human drama, asking me to mingle with the fog that covers the valley below. Like the giant Firs standing at the water's edge, I stand in silence, listening to the river's cleansing flow. For one infinite moment, I become the trees, seeing all that has passed before. Then, through the fog, my senses are pierced with clarity. I have heard the eternal pattern. It contains the music of all life forms and breathes in unison with the heartbeat of every living thing.

In that eternal moment, while hearing the pattern, the fog lifts and my heart is touched by the light of Grandfather Sun.

HEARING THE HEART'S VISION
✖

When we listen and *hear* the small, still voice within our hearts, we can access our greatest potential joy and desire. This is the heart's vision—the personal dream that will allow the individual to accomplish the things that bring happiness and fulfillment.

When we hear the heart's voice and fling our deepest longings and desires toward that heart vision, the body and senses merely follow the heartstrings that are made from our faith. This is the magic of personal creation and manifestation that marks the wholehearted seeker who knows that miracles are real. This individual creates the miracle of cooperation through the faith and willingness to be a partner with the Great Mystery, allowing personal desire to manifest in its own way.

By flinging our dreams and greatest desires, attached to the red heartstrings of faith, into the Void of the Unknown, we show our trust in the Maker. The harvest we reap shows our faith in ourselves and our joyful connection to the Great Mystery.

THE QUIET MIND
✂

Caution,
There is a silence.
A stillness, deep within.
An absence of patterns,
Where light and shadow blend.
Hearken,
To the darkness
Of the Void of the Unknown.
Hearing
Total nothingness
That thunders all alone.
Travel into the pulsing of
Silent time or space.
The quiet mind
brings calmness,
Infinite, eternal grace.
Born inside silence,
Is the will—to be.
Chaos becoming order,
The holiness of life—
The unfolding of Great Mystery.

LISTENING WITH THE OTHER SENSES

The pleading eyes of a child can speak a thousand words. The bent and broken body of an Elder speaks of a hard life. The lines of pain in the face of another human being can speak of burdens carried for many years. Many people in these conditions may not feel safe enough to speak of their pain or know how to release the weight of their burdens.

Silence and patience can open the space that allows another to express those feelings that have been shut off. The timid ones who have born the brunt of abuse use many other means of subtle communication to relay their feelings. The shy ones may have been silenced by those around them who were so involved in their own anger that the fury of feelings left no space for another's expression.

The wise individual looks and hears the unspoken signals that scream for the need to be recognized. The gentle and sensitive listener is adept at the art of creating safety and a space for sharing that allows others to express their needs. This kind of listener observes the subtle language of the heart within others, respecting the appropriate timing needed for the trust to be present between the speaker and the listener. Hearing with the eyes, nose, ears, and heart of the spirit is how the astute listener reaches out to others, allowing healing to occur.

DEFENDING WITH WORDS
✄

Defending every personal viewpoint without allowing another to respond is the act of an insecure person. Having to accuse in order to be right or accusing another of making others wrong is based in fear. The act of projecting one's personal insecurities on others is a human trait. The astute listener can detect exactly what needs to be healed when a person is defending their *right to be* through using these means.

It is not appropriate to volunteer to assist in correcting this type of behavior in another. The offer will always be met with further justifications of why that person is right. This precarious situation can only be corrected when the speaker's *internal* self-rejection and self-criticism is confronted and healed by that individual. To offer advice or methods to heal this type of self-hatred is a waste of energy. The healing will occur in its own time and is between the individual and the Great Mystery. This healing occurs when the person defending with words makes a conscious choice to change the insecure, self-important "I," making a partnership with the Creator to the eternal "we."

Listening Woman, the Clan Mother of the Fifth Moon Cycle, hears our struggle when we defend with words. She knows how hard it is to surrender the self-important yet insecure ego to the Great Mystery. It may be time to ask ourselves how often we feel disconnected, allowing the chatter of our mind's criticism to make us feel unwanted or unloved. It may be time to make a conscious choice to let that behavior go and to ask for the strength it takes to love ourselves and others without judgment and with sensitivity.

LISTENING WOMAN
⚌

Echoes of the Ancestors
Ride the Winds of Change,
Voices of the Creatures
Calling out my name.
Singing spirits on the breeze,
The crashing of waves to shore,
The pounding of Earth Mother's heart,
Teach me what to listen for.
In stillness, before dusk and dawn,
Hidden messages are set free.
Like the chants of my People,
Their rhythms speak to me.
My ears can hear this music,
And my heart can understand.
Clan Mother of Tiyoweh,
I am yours to command.
I listen for your whispers
On a course you will chart,
Searching for the still voice
That lives within my heart.

Listening Woman, the Clan Mother of the Fifth Moon Cycle, teaches us that all human beings have the potential to hear the still voice within their hearts. We know this voice by the serenity it makes us feel and the joy that fills us when we follow the messages it gives. The heart's voice leads us to the place of inner peace where we are in harmony with who and what we are. This place of inner knowing and at-one-ment cannot be taken away. When we seek the heart's voice, we reside in the safety of being serenely balanced and feeling marvelously alive. The Ancestors called it Tiyoweh, the Stillness. Those who seek it will always find it within.

THE UNBRIDLED RESPONSE OF INNOCENCE
✖

All people who have the sensitivity to really hear what is happening around them warm to the unbridled response of innocence. The child who looks deep into your eyes, trusting you enough to ask a question, whose answer you know could make the needed difference in that young life. The excitement of the elderly, when they have been told that someone remembered to visit them, just when they thought they had been forgotten. The pleasure of learning that has come to the illiterate when they realize they *can* make sense out of the marks and scribbles they have seen but never understood.

Unbridled response of any kind makes us sit up and pay attention, but the simple and joyful giggles, laughter, and "Oh, my's" of innocence are remembered all of our days. To think that these sounds can write a million indelible messages across our hearts is to understand why caring people find such happiness in giving to others.

If you would like to hear the unbridled responses of innocence, making them some of your treasured memories, it may be time to give of yourself—especially when it is unexpected.

SPIRITUAL GRATIFICATION

When we look at all of the kinds of spiritual gratification that humankind can receive, these could fill entire libraries, if they were
recorded as personal experiences. We are filled with Spirit every
time we become inspired by something we hear, observe, think,
read, touch, perceive, taste, smell, or remember.

These experiences allow us to hear our hearts pounding, to
feel the quick intake of breath, to measure the differences in how we
feel, and to remember the specialness of these moments in our lives.

For some, the silent compassion and gentle touch of someone
who cares inspires them to take courage. In all instances, the silent,
yet thundering rush of inspiration can be heard through the human
senses—as long as we are willing to hear through using our sensitivity. This ability comes from letting go of the mental armor we
use to protect this same sensitive vulnerability. Our spirits are then
grateful for being allowed to digest the inspiration that feeds them.

TRANQUILLITY
✣

TRANQUILLITY—THE PERFECT REMEDY FOR
TOO MUCH HUMAN INTERACTION!

If you have been the sponge for every loud conversation, blaring television, sad story, ringing phone, and silly argument in your range of experience, *take a break!* There are times when the faucet of human interaction needs to be cut off.

One of my wise Grandmother teachers used to talk to me about rocking out the frustration in the front porch rocking chair. I thought it curious at the time when there was nothing outside but a seemingly unchanging view of the desert. She told me that the motion gets people back into the rhythm of tranquillity. Being twenty-two, I didn't really understand. Her words are treasures to me now. We can find the rhythms of tranquillity in the gentle sameness of the rocking chair. In these rhythms, we can do Grandma Cisi's favorite thing—"set our minds to relaxing."

HEARTBEAT OF WHOLENESS

IT IS A RARE BREED OF HUMAN WHO CAN
BLEND A FREE SPIRIT, A DECISIVE NATURE,
A DEEP RESPECT FOR LIFE, LOVE FOR
ADVENTURE, AND AN UNCOMPROMISING
SENSE OF INTEGRITY INTO PERSONAL HAPPINESS.
SUCH INDIVIDUALS HEAR THE HEARTBEAT
OF WHOLENESS.

Nothing is impossible when we are dealing with human potential. We can hear the heartbeat of wholeness, never knowing what it is that leads us toward our desired goals. We can simply be doing what feels right to us, and we will be using the heartbeat of wholeness as our natural rhythm.

We have been taught by the technical society that we live in that most things are complex. If we believe this, it becomes true. It may be time for all of us to use the hearing that exists without sound. When we trust the soundless feelings, we can hear the wholeness that leads us to personal happiness.

LEARNING OBEDIENCE
❌

Nothing stirs the rebel
Like having to obey
All of the signposts that
Guide the Beauty Way.

Nothing makes the ego fear
The point of no return
Like the idea of obeying
The inner voice of concern.

Nothing fills the heart
Like the spirit on the wind,
Reflecting truthful answers,
Like the guidance of a friend.

When we honor the sacred whispers
Of the small, still voice of will,
Our obedience becomes a pleasure,
Our realized dreams reflect our skill.

The voice of will is our deepest desire for wholeness. To ignore this voice courts disaster; to obey our will is to become synchronistic. What do you hear your small, still voice saying?

LESSONS OF THE CREATURES' CALLS

✖

No Trails was a great tracker and hunter among his people. He had earned his name because he could locate any person or beast that roamed the Earth. His uncanny ability to see what was not apparent, and to hear the calls of the creatures when no one else was able to, allowed him to follow the invisible trails that led him to his goal.

One morning, No Trails was deep in the high meadows of the mountains that bordered his homeland, silently passing through the naked aspens. He motioned the man beside him to be silent, not moving. His companion, Drinks the Sun, had not noticed Mother Grizzly Bear or her cubs until No Trails motioned with his chin. They stood and watched as a fight ensued between Mama Bear and a renegade male who had wandered into her territory. The sounds were bone-shaking as the bears fought for the right to claim a downed deer as their food. The cubs scampered up trees and were wailing in fear until Mama ran the old rogue off.

Back at camp that night, Drinks the Sun learned something new. No Trails explained that the Great Mystery did not give human beings any common calls like the creatures. The Creator blessed the human beings with the gifts of being able to listen, and to mimic the calls of their Creature Relations. Creator had a plan for ensuring that humankind would never forget to listen, and to learn the languages of the Creature-teachers. Without understanding these sounds, human beings would never see the value of survival instinct.

Believe it or not, our survival does depend on how we listen. Are you hearing what life is asking of you?

PENSIVE SILENCE
⚹

> TO DENY THE NEED FOR SILENT
> REFLECTION IS TO DENY THE
> THOUGHT PROCESS THAT GIVES
> LIFE ITS NEEDED PERSPECTIVE.

In pensive silence, the mind calms enough to review and to sort out the feelings, perceptions, events, ideas, and conversations of the day. The Elders say that this is one reason why Great Mystery divided the light into day and night. Activities are reserved for daytime. Sunset brings the quiet time for thoughts. We are then able to replay our memories of the day's activities. During the night that follows, we are able to dream the results of our reflections into workable solutions to enhance our lives.

It must be a human trait to forget that we listen to our thoughts, our ideas, and our memories as much as we feel them or see them in our mind's eye. The thought process is most potent when we use all of our senses, creating and recreating the smallest nuance that could give new meaning to the whole picture.

If you have not been allowing yourself the time needed for pensive silence, confusion may be knocking at your door. Is it time to sort things out by listening to what is being replayed through your memories of today?

HONORING EVERY PERSON
✂

In ancient times, Native Ancestors honored every kind of human being. There was no judgment against the ones who had other than heterosexual sexual preferences, the ones who were eccentric, or the ones who were *touched* with hearing voices.

The nonlogical or different behaviors of others were accepted because our Medicine People understood that all people are exactly where they are supposed to be, doing whatever that entails. The experiences of any life are a mystery that the Creator has given people so that they may learn. The Ancestors' practice of noninterference allowed each person to act out these lessons to the fullest.

Those who heard voices and talked to unseen spirits often came up with very unusual and workable solutions for Tribal problems. These *touched* individuals did not operate from the same logical viewpoint that blocked others from seeing nonlogical solutions. Many times the lives of these individuals were considered Holy because they stood in both worlds at the same time, the spiritual, or nontangible, world and the natural world.

Is our lesson in this modern era to let go of our judgments about nonlogical behavior? Or is our lesson to let go of our fear of hearing voices? In all instances, we can learn a lot if we listen. Who knows, if you pass people in the street who are talking to imaginary friends, listen—the message they speak may be for you!

FEAR OF SILENCE
✖

In every part of humankind, we find people who are afraid of silence, or so it would seem. Some people love to talk, just to hear the sound of their own voices. Others talk because they are self-conscious, uncomfortable, or nervous. Some people talk from insecurity, needing to tell you why you should think they are great, really trying to convince themselves. When any person talks without allowing others to speak, and then does not listen when another gets a chance to reply, the talker is afraid of silence.

The fear of silence is most prevalent in cultures that feel that people need to be entertained, or in cultures that do not consider silence or quiet reflection a virtue. Fear of silence usually comes when people have a lot of negative chatter in the mind. When they are talking, the mental criticism cannot run simultaneously.

Astute listeners pick up the warning signals and realize that they will lose energy if they stay to listen to the fearful person's incessant chatter. A good listener really hears what a person is saying and is not thinking of what the reply should be. It takes a great deal of energy to be authentically present and truthfully listening. Such listeners have a quiet mind and a very good memory because they are only hearing the conversation, not talk mixed with other thoughts of their own.

If you feel uncomfortable reading this, you may want to work on the parts that keep you from being a good listener, or any fear of silence you may have. We can all use work on being authentically present, hearing and remembering what is said.

INNER POTENTIAL

In the swampy glades that surrounded the lake, the little girl listened intently before stepping off the foot-beaten path. There were many creatures who lived near the water that could harm human beings. Thus, caution and listening were the first lessons the children of the Tribe were taught.

Blue Bell was returning from the lake with the water her mother had requested, when she heard a voice in her head. It did not sound like her own voice, which related her thoughts to what she was experiencing, and so she stopped in her tracks.

Night fell, and the warriors finally found her. They took the little girl to the Medicine Woman because she was pale and disoriented. After a gourd of healing herbal tea, she could speak. The Medicine Woman asked what happened, and Blue Bell told of hearing the voice. The voice had spoken of many things that could happen in Blue Bell's life. The Medicine Woman encouraged the child by being silent and nodding until the story was complete.

The Wise Woman told Blue Bell and her anxious mother that all was as it should be. The voice had told the child about her inner potential. The voice had given the little girl a map that would allow her to fulfill the mission she had come to accomplish. This was no voice from another spirit; this was the voice of Blue Bell's inner potential. Being a child and not being afraid to listen, Blue Bell had done what few adults would do. She stopped, and she heard the small, still voice within.

INVESTING IN HARMONY

Investing in the harmony
We want to rule our lives
Comes by making the effort
To listen, and then realize:
Just one discordant comment
Can wreak havoc to the whole,
Shattering precious harmony,
Or the serenity of the soul.
Listening to the talk of others,
Then listening to our own,
Allows us vivid comparisons,
Of all the seeds we've sown.
Gossip breeds ugly judgments,
And lies can bring us pain,
The negativity we listen to
Kills the harmony we've attained.
In listening to bitter resentment,
Or hearing jealousy used to defame,
By refusing to stop the speaker,
The listener is also to blame.
Harmony is an investment,
Fed with each thought and deed,
We can choose to Walk in Beauty,
Or let discord take the lead.

HEARING THE TOTEMS
✂

In ancient times, our legends say that the creatures spoke to human beings. It is not clear to modern-day humans whether this was metaphor or not. The skeptic would assure us that it was a fairy-tale legend. How can it be explained to the pseudo-intellectual, that hearing comes from knowing many different kinds of languages and ways to listen?

We can hear the animals' voices when they are wounded, their screams reflecting agony and pain. In any nature biologist's field recordings, we can hear the difference in their mating calls and their warning calls. Human beings can mimic the creatures' voices, and hunters can bring them to any area with replicas of these sounds. The Totems' call is different though; the messages are silent.

The Totems' consciousness is the essential spirit of the entire Tribe of that species. It cannot be heard with the ears; it is a living spirit that aligns with a human being and speaks to that person's inner knowing. Some may hear it as a voice in their own minds, while others feel the messages form as emotions that urge them to follow a certain path. Some people hear their Totems through seeing pictures in their minds and must then intuit the meaning of those visions. To invalidate the message, or the way we perceive it, is to ignore the language of the Totems. Messages from the Totems have to be experienced firsthand; otherwise, it is merely a myth to anyone who has forgotten how to hear Spirit.

6TH MOON

PERCEIVING LIFE IN CONCEPTS

Native children are taught by their Elders to see life in relationship to all things. Many other cultures see life in a linear fashion. Through stories that reflect relationship, Indian children are taught about the interdependency of all living things. When all human beings can grasp the conceptional idea of the Circles of life forms and relationships that make up the whole of Creation, we will be able to understand the purpose of harmony.

One way that the pieces of the seemingly discordant puzzle can come together is through storytelling. Stories show people how problems are worked out and lessons are learned. We expand our viewpoints when we learn how other cultures do things, we see similarities between ways of living, and we grow through finding and using the common thread that makes us a planetary family. Every part of Creation depends on every other part—even if we cannot see how these relationships work in harmony.

Storyteller, the Clan Mother of the Sixth Moon Cycle, teaches us how to trust these connections to all things. This Clan Mother gives us stories that point to our place in the whole and show us our correct relationship to all life forms. When we find our place, we find ways we can use our skills to make our bodies, hearts, minds, and spirits strong. From that inner strength, humans can take their places as generous Guardians of precious Earth resources.

THE CHILD AND GRANDMOTHER MOON
❇

Grandmother,
Teach me how to touch the stars,
To give the sky a smile,
To wait for the rainbow after the storm.
And I will share with you
The laughter in my eyes,
The warmness of my love,
The trust within my heart,
And the innocence of my greatest joy—
Knowing I am watched over by you.

Storyteller, the Clan Mother of the Sixth Moon Cycle, can paint the picture of the child within every human being and bring us back to that magical place so that we may remember through our feelings. How long has it been since you remembered the smells, textures, sounds, and tastes of something that was good in your childhood?

TALES THAT NEED TELLING

✂

Storytellers hold a place of respect in Indian Nations because of the truthful solutions laced in their tales that can be applied to any situation at any point in time. The spoken truth, based in ancient wisdom, stands apart from the apparentness that "times have changed."

When we forget the truths that gave courage and strength to the Ancestors of all races and creeds, we have lost ourselves and our roots.

It may be time to seek out the stories that formed the ancient connections to your Ancestors—every bloodline you carry. Then you may find a new inner strength, well-being, and sense of worth.

SPEAKING THE TRUTHS OF THE PAST
✂

The rivers of myth, the rivers of legend, and the rivers of history flow in many directions. Each river holds the viewpoint of a certain race, Tribe, or Nation and captures the flow of life that each believed to be the truth.

Where all waters of truth converge is the delta of Remembering—the place where the truth touches every heart. The truths that bring the Remembering are spoken by the Storyteller. When the listeners' hearts are opened to new understandings through ancient teachings, the spirit grows. To weave these stories that teach humankind to grasp the truths of the whole is a rare gift.

What would happen to the personal stories and memories of the Elders you hold dear if you do not ask and record these stories?

If you were suddenly taken from your family through accident or illness, what would you have wanted them to know about your personal history? Before any disaster threatens, is it time to leave a legacy that will be a source of strength and joy to the next generations of your family?

VISITORS IN ANOTHER'S LAND
✖

Native Americans have many unspoken rules of conduct. The improper manners of an uninformed guest have frustrated Indian people for years because the host is usually not willing to correct a visitor for a breach of etiquette. The standards of proper behavior are taught from the time a child is old enough to walk and are so ingrained that natural respect for others simply becomes a way of being.

When we are guests in another's home or in another's land, we are required to follow the Tribal Traditions of that land in order to show respect to our hosts. If we do not know these Traditions, we ask permission before doing anything. It is proper to offer to help with the work involved getting meals, doing chores, and cleaning. We never carry feathers or other Medicines with us when visiting. The same things that bring us strength may offend another or their Tradition.

We never look in drawers or closets, or pick up any object without permission. We do not eavesdrop or observe any disagreement, removing ourselves to allow privacy for others. We stay out of anything that is not our business. We never assume—we ask.

We never do a Ceremony on land that is not our own without being invited or receiving permission from the local Elder or Medicine Person of that area. These are simple rules of respect that show our gratitude for being hosted by others. Through respect, we honor the spirits that are the Guardians of others' lands as well as their customs and their Ancestors.

STORY OF REVENGE
✂

Mole was living in the forest, burrowing into the hill, when he heard the screams of his family. Hurrying home, he found the forest ablaze and heard from other fleeing creatures that Coyote had started the fire.

Mole's family had not survived. Mole's anger was so great that he made a vow to get revenge upon every Coyote he came upon, until the end of his days.

Mole killed many Coyotes over the years, shutting his ears to their pleading for their babies and shutting his eyes to their pain. In his old age, he came across another who had fled the forest on that day long ago. Mole was eager to gather more hateful information that would give his old bones the new vitality he needed to carry out his brutal revenge.

As Bluejay relayed all that had happened, a strange feeling came over Mole. Mole was sick. He wanted to die. He could not believe what he was hearing.

Later that night, as Grandmother Moon rose, Mole screamed his agony into the forest. Mole cried out to Earth Mother, and she answered him saying,

"Mole, you have finally heard the truth of Coyote's story. Coyote was burned alive trying to save your family from the fire that was started by lightning hitting a tree. From this day forward, you will be blinded by light, your ears will be bound to your head, and you will forever bear the symbols of your need for revenge."

*→ Grandmother moon's revenge?

153

HURRIED WORDS

The rush of explanation
Stifles the fullness to be gained,
When slick, unfounded patter
Seeks to befuddle the brain.
But words that speak of feelings,
And of the patterns we weave,
Leave all conclusions open,
Without trying to deceive.
Those who share their story
Are the messengers that we meet,
Who show us some alternatives,
Instead of bowing to defeat.
If we honor every speaker,
And the stories that they tell,
We may learn how to draw
From the depths of wisdom's well.

Every human being is a messenger of some kind; having to hurry the message leaves the listener in confusion. Time can make a difference. Only the wise take the time needed, never needing to explain. When have you forgotten explanations and simply stated your truth, not caring what others thought?

SPEAKING AND TRUST

Among Indian people in ancient times, some of the rules of etiquette regarding speaking were

> Never discuss another's business, and never presume to speak for anyone other than yourself.
>
> Respect the privacy of all people, and never break a trust if you have been told something in confidence.
>
> Never repeat ugly rumors about another, and remove yourself from any group or person speaking in that manner.
>
> Never offer advice unless it is asked for, and never discuss another's situation, as you see it, without permission.
>
> If someone is having a conversation or argument that does not concern you, leave the area; do not eavesdrop.
>
> Never bring your burdens into another's home by talking about your troubles, unless that person has agreed to be an adviser; then listen to the wisdom offered and take the advice given.
>
> Never tell a lie or half-truth, or alter any message that you are to deliver for another.

These rules were strictly adhered to by those who earned the respect of others in their Tribe. When anyone uses these rules of thumb, the words they speak are truthful and to be trusted. The level of integrity that is required to speak the truth in this manner is a rare find in the modern world. For their words to attain this level of respect, speakers must live in truth at all times.

CURRENTS OF THE RIVER

The currents of the river
Take me 'round each bend,
Over white-water rapids,
Until I begin to blend
With the Water Spirits.
As we journey on our way,
Past the shores of memories,
The sun dawns on today.
The flow of life engulfs me,
My passage, the river's sounds,
The currents take me safely,
'Til I stand on sacred ground.
The songs of the river
Still ring within my soul,
Asking me to sing with them,
As I stand upon the shoal.
"Allow all those around you
To follow their own trails,
Finding their uniquenesses,
And telling their own tales.
Every current is different,
Every lesson will unfold,
And the flow of each river,
Brings blessings to the soul."

HUMOR
✂

The laughter of happy hearts has healed a world of woes throughout time. Humor is one of the most powerful tools that the Creator has given humankind. The ability to laugh at ourselves has given the Human Tribe a way to shake off the seriousness that sometimes masks our arrogance and our fear. Indian people have used clowns—sometimes called Heyokah by the Lakota people or Koshari by the Hopi people—to play harmless jokes on their Tribes so that the laughter can balance the sacredness of a Ceremony with joy and irreverence.

This ancient custom is one way we can balance the sorrow and seriousness of human life. With the outpouring of belly laughs, nothing can stick that could harm or limit our ability to create. We can change our negative viewpoints in an instant with side-splitting laughter.

If you are taking yourself too seriously, you may want to try some Heyokah Moon Medicine. Go into your backyard at night, drop your drawers, and moon the world!

STORY OF THE TIDES
✖

The children sat above the sea, watching the ocean waves from the cliff, listening to the soft voice of a Grandmother spinning a tale. Grandmother showed the children the sounds of the tides that were living inside the shells in her basket, telling the little ones how the shells taught the Human Tribe how to listen to their feelings.

One of the curious little ones posed a question, and the Grandmother responded by taking the group to the shoreline. Along the way she had each child pick a flower. The Old One had the children throw their flowers into the sea, explaining that every feeling that each child felt would be sent into the world but would one day return to the sender.

The children watched as some flowers were drowned, others washed ashore, and some, which had not been thrown far enough, sat in the sand waiting to be taken out to sea by the incoming tide. The Old One explained that like the flowers on the shore, good feelings should be placed far enough into the seas of life to be shared, or the feelings could not come back to the sender as blessings. The flowers that drowned represented the bad feelings that needed to be cleansed by salty tears. Grandmother explained that the feelings that were meant to hurt others should not be sent into the world, because they, too, would eventually find their way back to the sender. The flowers that rode on the tops of the waves represented the powerful image of all of life's feelings. These feelings mirrored the laughter and the tears that were lovingly shared with others. These shared feelings flowed, like the rhythms of the seas, until the tides of understanding brought them back to the shore that the heart called home.

DEVOTION AND COMMITMENT
✖

TRUE DEVOTION AND COMMITMENT ARE NEVER
MADE WITH THE MIND. THESE QUALITIES, WHICH
ALLOW US TO EXPAND, TO GROW, AND TO BLOOM
INTO OUR POTENTIAL, ARE DEVELOPED THROUGH
THE HEART AND THE SPIRIT.

*Storyteller, the Clan Mother of the Sixth Moon Cycle, shows us many
lessons in how to overcome our challenges through the tales she tells. It is
the responsibility of the listeners to sort out which parts of the story apply
to them and can assist them in their personal expansion or growth. The
application of the truths that each individual finds in a story must be
coupled with devotion and commitment. The individual's heart and spirit
must desire change and personal betterment.*

*Is it time to ask yourself if you have buried the desire of the heart and
spirit in the busy life you lead? Or has your lack of desire brought boredom and apathy? Could it be time to free the heart and spirit from a self-
imposed prison built from disappointments? Let the past go and begin
again in the present by seeking any part of your personal dream you
gave away through lack of devotion and commitment to that dream.*

FRIENDSHIP
✖

Friends show us many things about how we are reacting to ourselves. The truthful words of a friend are rare treasures that cannot be bought or sold. A real friend speaks the truth in a manner that supports our growth, never choosing to degrade or minimize who we are. A friend accepts the rough edges that we carry and allows us to add polish at our own time and in our own way. A valued friend has the sensitivity to speak to us in a way that urges us to be the best we can personally be, without insisting upon perfection.

Those who are not friends to themselves find themselves with a multitude of acquaintances that will vanish with the first sign of stormy waters. The lack of sensitivity that these troubled people show others is merely a reflection of how they are internally treating themselves. The inability to speak the truth to the Self destroys the potential of friendship between the Self and another. Integrity and sensitivity toward the Self allows one to draw others of high values into the circle of friendship that has its basis in trust. If we can trust what we think and direct toward ourselves, we can learn to trust the sensitive words and thoughts presented to us by another.

Storyteller, the Clan Mother of the Sixth Moon Cycle, reminds us of the mirror reflection that exists in every act of life. If we are seemingly being attacked by others, it is a reflection of what we are internally doing to ourselves with our own negative thoughts. Once we choose to stop the self-hatred, self-criticism, and self-rejection, the attacks stop happening in our life experience. Is it time to catch these negative, internal thoughts and to change them, finding something you can admire about you?

APOLOGIES

Apologies come easily
To the insincere,
Who never count the cost of
The words that brought the tears.
Apologies are never heard
From the ones who blame
All others for their actions,
Instead of being ashamed.
The stubborn and self-righteous
Refuse to yield or to obey
The quiet voice of conscience
That knows the healing way.
Words hold much power,
And we can choose to use
Our words as swords of anger,
Counted by the love we lose.
Our sincere apology comes
When our words have been unfair,
And our hearts can recognize
Another's feelings in need of repair.
Standing as the recipient of
Our thoughtless actions or words
Gives us a new perspective on
An apology—sincere and well deserved.

THE PEACE TREE
✄

Great branches of the White Pine shaded the ground below as Woodpecker gave the Peace Tree a good cleaning. Woodpecker was eating the little insects that had come to feast on the inner bark. It felt good to be cleansed of the creepy-crawlers that had gotten under the Peace Tree's skin. From time to time, it was necessary for White Pine to call on Woodpecker to perform this act of service. Even the Peace Tree had experiences that were a bother.

Woodpecker found joy in eating the juicy bugs that had plagued his friend, White Pine. He realized that his mission of service was to protect the peace by ridding White Pine, who was the Peacekeeper of the forest, of unwanted distractions. To this day, the feathers of Flicker, the Woodpecker, are highly prized for the strength of their cleansing of negativity and for their protection.

Storyteller, the Clan Mother of the Sixth Moon Cycle, shows us that anything we allow to get under our skin detracts from our ability to find inner peace. The judgmental words of others can reflect our need for outside approval. We can protect ourselves from the unjust opinions of others through cleansing the negativity, adjusting our focus, and allowing the Peace Tree to be our teacher. Is something bothering you that should be cleansed in order for you to rediscover and to protect your inner peace?

STORYTELLER
✂

Tell me a story, sweet Mother,
Of the Ancestors and their days,
Of how they Walked with Beauty,
Learning the Medicine Ways.

As you relate the stories,
I am allowed to see
The importance of every lesson
And how it applies to me.

Through another's example,
I share the laughter and the tears.
Through another's experience,
I learn how love can conquer fear.

Together we can journey
Through those other times,
Reclaiming all the wisdom
Of the legacies left behind.

Storyteller, the Clan Mother of the Sixth Moon Cycle, reminds us that if we are willing to expand, growing beyond our former zone of comfort in a healthy way, we must pay attention to all of the events in our lives. There is a story connected to every living thing and every person in our world. How that story influences our personal Earthwalks is determined by our willingness to see another's experience as a way to learn about ourselves. We can become so self-obsessed that we never hear or see the opportunities surrounding us. We can be so numbed or broken by the burdens we carry that we are oblivious to the rest of life going on around us. To unravel the confusion, Storyteller asks us to see the similarities in ourselves and others, finding ways to learn from the stories we all share in common.

TRUTH TELLING
✖

HAVING THE *AUDACITY* TO TELL THE TRUTH IN
THE FACE OF OPPOSITION AND CHAOS, IN THE
COMPANY OF THOSE WHO LIVE WITH CONSTANT,
SELF-CREATED DECEPTION, IS THE MARK OF A
PEACEMAKER.

The choice to dare to speak the truth comes hard for those who
fear retribution or lack of acceptance. The person who has made
peace with the Self, becoming accountable for his or her own actions, finds the truth easy to speak. Telling the truth becomes a way
of being, rather than a dreaded experience. Learning to tell the truth
in all situations allows the speaker to be free from having to cover
former lies with more deceptions. Peacemakers don't have to wage
the war of fighting the enemy within; truthfulness has dissolved
their inner conflicts. Is it time to apply the truth to some turmoil in
your life?

SPEAKING WITH AUTHORITY
✄

The person who speaks with authority usually knows what she or he is about. Such speakers can use that authority to try to sway others into accepting their point of view. This is not to say that every person who speaks with authority has the best interests of others in mind.

True authority comes from the experience of having lived with our decisions, not asking others to do anything our way, but rather presenting another point of view. When we speak from our personal experiences and truths, our voices carry a certain ring of authenticity. This is the sound of sincerity found in the pure of heart.

There is no substitute for openhearted truth. There is no better way to communicate than speaking *only* of what one has experienced firsthand. Anything else is hearsay, someone else's opinion, or an intellectual belief. When we speak from the things we know and are willing to listen to the things others know from their experience, we open our senses to learning. When all that we talk about is what we've read or heard another expound upon, we lose the magic of experiencing these things ourselves. This kind of small talk is for the sideline observer of life. The people who are actively playing the game of life have hard-earned authority. The balance is found when the thinkers also become dedicated players.

ORIGINALITY AND TRADITION
✂

The group of young mothers who wanted to become storytellers sat quietly as Storyteller explained the manner in which some stories became traditional favorites.

"We all have our favorite stories that bring us memories of what we learned from those tales as we were growing up. Few of us have ever taken the time to think of how these stories evolved. The first storyteller who created the oldest of tales must have had a great talent for originality. The old stories, which taught us ways to grow, have endured to become parts of our Traditions.

"The stories that lacked inspired creativity and originality have been forgotten because they did not speak to the listeners' hearts. That is the way of Tradition. We keep the goodness that teaches us how to grow, the purity that guides us in times of trouble, and the originality of thought that shows the human beings how to conquer the challenges in life. We discard the things that no longer make sense, or cannot answer the needs of the People.

"When a new idea or story comes along that applies to changing times, we should show our gratitude. These new solutions become important, especially when the story's answers help our young people. As the years pass, this so-called new tale earns being called Traditional, even though the origin is not as old as some other teachings. So I never want you young women to forget that your insight and originality give birth to what our future generations will call Traditional wisdom."

FRUITFUL CULTURES
✂

*The fruits of any culture
Lie in the tales they weave,
Giving their inspiration,
Without trying to deceive.
The tale that tells of courage
Invites us to be brave.
The tale that tells of waste
Shows the reckless how to save.
The tale that tells of consequence
Brings warnings to the wise.
The tale that asks us questions
Urges solutions we devise.
The tale that speaks of true love
Asks our hearts to open wide.
The tale that tells of victories
Restores our human pride.
When these truths are woven
With the greatest of human care,
The lessons we can harvest
May be answers to our prayers.
Those who weave the stories
Are an inspiration to humankind,
Harvesting the fruits of wisdom
And offering food for the mind.*

TESTING THE TRUTH

IRREVERENCE IS ONE WAY THAT THE
DIVINE TRICKSTER, WHO LIVES INSIDE
ALL OF US, CAN TEST THE TRUTHS OF
ANY PHILOSOPHY, RELIGION, OR BODY
OF KNOWLEDGE.

The philosophy, religion, or way of life that contains no humor cannot survive. The lack of laughter or the ability to have good, clean fun is a red flag warning that something is amiss. We can test the truths that we wish to embrace by being irreverent. When the time is appropriate, cut loose! If the crazy antics of playfulness are not acceptable to the serious-minded people who espouse the truth of their particular philosophy, pay attention, then run like hell. Although most Native Traditions don't have a concept for hell, the lack of laughter and irreverence would be close enough!

VANISHING CULTURES
><

Human life on our planet is a shared dream. When the legends, myths, and stories are allowed to die, the basic values of life deteriorate. The dreams of any culture are based upon the role models of legend. Not having any larger-than-life role models when the tales vanish, the following generations of any culture lose their drive to excel. When there is nothing to aspire to, dreams die hard, leaving the shared planetary dream resembling a nightmare.

Native American chronicles of oral legend and myth are called Medicine Stories. These stories are like Medicine to our culture. Through the revival of our Ancient Teachings, our children are finding their own Medicines—their gifts and abilities.

The tales of harmony and honesty, sharing and valor, loving and forgiving, come alive when the Medicine Stories are told. When the basic values of harmonious living are told and retold, heroes and heroines come to life, becoming treasured teachers and friends. When the Wise Ones go silent, the dreams of the young wither, being replaced by the unhealthy values on the street. Without the storytellers, entire cultures can pass into oblivion.

Is it time to find the myths of your genetic ancestry? It may be time to identify with the heroes and heroines that represent your culture. What a wonderful gift it would be for your children, teaching them the strength of their roots. If you do not have children, do it for yourself, and see how those stories can give you understanding of some part of yourself. You may find that you carry the same needs of today's youth; discovering who you are and where your roots come from gives strength to any growing individual.

SWALLOWED SOUNDS

Has No Voice was a mystery to the Medicine People of her Tribe. She had never spoken. The long years of silence had convinced her family that she would never utter a word. The child heard and was able to communicate through hand signs, but everyone had lost hope that she would ever sing or raise her voice in thanksgiving during Ceremony.

It was certain that Has No Voice's childhood had been strange. She was born under a stand of willows where her mother had gone to bring her into the world. The first hours of her young life were fraught with horrible events when her Tribe's camp was raided by their nearest enemy's war party. Has No Voice's father found them and protected them, losing his life in the process.

One day, in her seventh winter of life, Has No Voice was taken ill. She had eaten some bad food and was retching. The Medicine Man was called. As Has No Voice felt her stomach convulse, a curious thing happened. Sounds came up with the rotten meal. More sounds came out of her as the astounded members of her family heard the cries of wounded and fearful people. The Holy Man smiled, as he explained that as a newborn she had swallowed the sounds, knowing that if she cried, she and her mother would die. The stomachache had allowed her to throw up her fear and to heal. Has No Voice earned a new name when she reclaimed her gift of speech; now she is called Has No Fear.

HARMONIOUS SPEAKING
✖

INTELLIGENCE, BUILT ON PROFOUND
SENSITIVITY, IS THE GIFT THAT ALLOWS
ANY INDIVIDUAL TO SPEAK WITH
HARMONY.

Speaking with truth is not too difficult a lesson to learn when one is honest with the Self. The art of speaking harmoniously is a bit more difficult because most people who are honest and direct tend to forget that brutal honesty is not always appreciated. If sensitivity is used, we never need to water down our meaning or the truth. When sensitivity is partnered with intelligence, we are using our powers of perception to notice where we can bring harmony into potentially upsetting situations. Respecting the vulnerability of those who trust us to be honest *and* gentle is the key to the art of speaking the truth in harmony.

If you have noticed the shocked faces of others when you have been too abrupt or insensitive, it might be time to temper your words. Stand in the shoes of others and ask yourself if you would take offense at your own manner of speaking. If you are sitting on the other side of this situation, give a copy of this page to the offender. Having been the offender and the offended, my permission to copy this page is granted!

ETERNAL FLAWS

><

THE UNIVERSE IS FLAWLESS, EVOLVING
AT ITS OWN HARMONIOUS RHYTHM,
WITH RAW CREATIVE FORCE GUIDING
ITS EVERY MOVE.

The only eternal flaws in this universe seem to be found in the way human beings insist on seeing Creation through the eyes of limitation. Maybe that is one reason faith came into being. If we can't see the overview for ourselves, noticing that the whole is flawless, we need faith to take us beyond our limitations. Even that human frailty has a perfect place in the Divine Plan. Perhaps the Great Mystery's intent was to confound the human mind so we could learn to trust—instead of trying to reason and figure it out!

After all, everything and every force in our universe is basically balanced and neutral. It is the human species that judges every feeling, event, experience, person, or thought as being good or bad. Maybe through faith and trust we can stop labeling and begin to look at life as just *being*.

DEFEATED BY AGE?

*Her old bones creaked
And her pace was slow,
But her smile was blindingly bright.
Her mind was sharp,
And her voice was kind,
Her manner was a true delight.*

*The world had changed
In the winters she'd known,
But she bore their weight with pride.
She shared her wisdom
And passed the goodness on,
Using her love of life as her guide.*

*She did not bow to time,
Using life as her stage,
She sought each morning's joy,
And she was never defeated by age.*

If we let go of our vain attempts to hide the winters we have passed, and embrace the idea of our hearts and minds being forever young, we may finally realize that attitude is everything!

EMPTYING THE BURDEN BASKET

Deep in the woodlands that surrounded the vast series of lakes, Night Moon trudged up the last hill that led to her Tribe's camp, carrying wood for the fire. It was not the wood her family would use, it was wood for another family whose members had fallen ill. The muscles in her legs were trembling with the effort of having made seven such trips on this day. She was cold in the pale afternoon sun, with the late autumn winds nearly freezing the perspiration on her body.

When she arrived at camp, she was met by her Grandmother and Grandfather. Their pained expressions told her that she was going to hear something she might not be happy with. Grandfather approached Night Moon, so she mustered the last of her strength to adjust the burden basket full of wood and stood as tall as her spasming muscles would allow.

"Granddaughter, we need to talk. You have seen to the needs of many, and never once did you ask for help from other young people who were still healthy. You have always been independent, helpful, and resourceful. That makes us proud of you, but you have forgotten the Great Mystery's lessons of balance. You are the only remaining member of our family who has not died from the sickness. We want you to remember that you are human. The Creator put many humans here, so that we could help one another. Saying that you need others to share your burden of helping the many is not shameful. There are many different ways that humans are forced to learn how to receive. Are you willing to empty your burden basket *before* you become ill?"

THE OPEN MIND
✖

THE MIND THAT CONTAINS NO FIXED JUDGMENTS
KNOWS AUTHENTIC HUMILITY. THE MASKS OF
SELF-IMPORTANCE DO NOT CONTROL THOSE WHO
ALLOW OTHERS TO SPEAK THEIR TRUTHS WITHOUT
ANY OVERT OR COVERT CRITICISM. THE HUMAN
BEING WHO HAS THIS TYPE OF OPEN MIND IS DEVOID
OF CARRYING OR DEVELOPING ANY TYPE OF
SUPERIOR ATTITUDE.

Have you ever noticed that the people who hold others in contempt, using condescending behavior, are unable to hide their critical opinions and must voice their contempt? Have you ever noticed that those who espouse their beliefs, making others wrong for theirs, always carry a self-righteous attitude? Have you ever noticed that those who speak softly, being generous with their praise of others, are open to new ideas and are at peace with themselves?

Is it time to see how open your mind can become, by casting aside your judgments? The reward of this kind of healing is authentic humility.

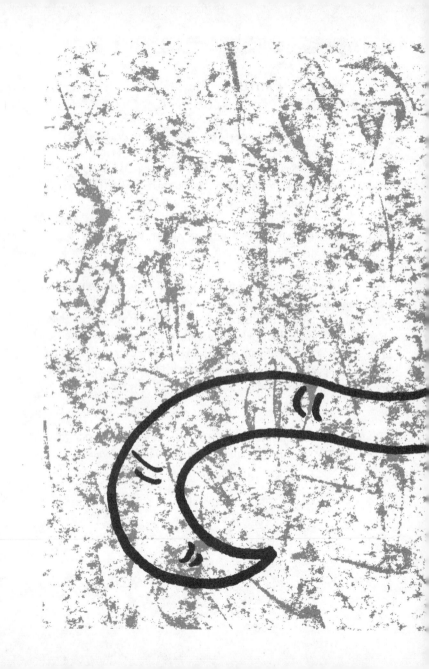

7TH
MOON

LOVING BEYOND FEAR

Swennio, Great Mystery,
You are the All-unfolding.
Teach me how to trust
My heart,
My feelings,
My inner knowing,
The senses of my body,
The blessings of my spirit.

These are the things
That urge me to love
Beyond my fear,
Trusting that forgiveness
Buries the hatchet of
Separation,
So that I may Walk in Beauty
With the passing
Of each glorious Sun.

The Clan Mother of the Seventh Moon Cycle, Loves All Things, teaches us to honor all of the senses of the body and the spirit as equal. In this manner, we can bring the marriage of Father Sky and Mother Earth into our bodies. When the heavens (our spiritual natures) and the Earth (our physical natures) are in harmony inside of our Sacred Spaces, we will Walk in Beauty. From this sense of harmony, we see the whole of Creation as an opportunity to learn and grow.

The bridge of forgiveness takes us across the abyss of self-imposed separation and we learn to give away our hurt and pain. Then the Earth Mother welcomes us home through transformative tears and shows us the healing path to wholeness.

FINDING LOVE WITHIN
✖

I taste the Red Earth
And acknowledge my humanness.
I feel the urge to create,
And my spirit soars
Like the spiraling hawk.
I touch the warmth
Of Grandfather Sun
So my heart will
Never grow cold.

Then I turn to the center
Of my Sacred Space,
Entering the Silence,
To rediscover the
Eternal Flame of Love.

The Great Mystery placed the Eternal Flame of Love in the center of every living thing. This flame is the connection that makes us all family and the glue that holds Creation together. When we touch that love inside of ourselves and share it with all of Creation by respecting each life form's right to be, we assure that our hearts will not grow cold.

Loves All Things, the Clan Mother of the Seventh Moon, guides us in the search of the human heart. She teaches us how to use respect, trust, and intimacy as the guidelines for all relationships. When we learn how to relate to others in this manner, we can turn and face ourselves, loving who and what we are, becoming our own best friend.

ALL ARE LOVED AS FAMILY
✖

Grandfather Sun shines on every creed and race. He does not limit his light to one variety of tree or one area of land. Grandmother Moon marks the passing of seasons and directs the flow of the tides for every Child of Earth. The Mother Earth nurtures every living thing and gives life abundant to all of the Earth Tribe. Father Sky houses the clouds, the thunder, the lightning, and the life-giving rains. The stones, plants, and creatures who are our Brothers and Sisters are here to teach us about being human. The Great Mystery set these creations in motion so all Two-legged humans could find their places in this family of All Our Relations.

It is time to honor this gift of family by taking our roles as Guardians of our resources. We are being asked to become the gentle caretakers that the Great Mystery intended us to be. The separation of the Fourth World is coming to an end. It is time. Now we must face the enemies that dwell within our hearts. The enemies of hatred and bitterness strangle our spirits and harden our hearts, telling us to cast aside the dream of planetary wholeness. Loves All Things shows us that we are one planet, one people, one race—the Human Tribe.

BURDENS OF THE SPIRIT WORLD
✂

AFTER DROPPING THE ROBE AND ACCEPTING PHYSICAL
DEATH, THE ONLY BURDEN HUMAN SPIRITS CARRY WITH
THEM INTO THE SPIRIT WORLD IS THE EMOTIONAL PAIN
THAT THEY CREATED BY REFUSING TO SHARE THEIR LOVE
WITH OTHERS DURING THEIR PHYSICAL LIFE.

Loves All Things, the Clan Mother of the Seventh Moon Cycle, reminds us that every moment of physical life is precious. Each human being in our lives is a rare living treasure that could instantly cease to be in our lives. This Clan Mother teaches us to never take any person or relationship for granted. Tell others how much you appreciate their love, support, humor, and companionship every day. There is no turning back the clock after they are gone. Regret is never necessary if we live our love and show our appreciation every day.

FOUNDATIONS
⬌

Foundations are the building blocks of all things found in the natural world. Foundations come in fours. The four cardinal directions, the four parts of a plant, the four seasons, and the four elements—air, earth, water, and fire. Everything we build in our lives has to have a foundation in order to survive.

The foundation of any successful relationship has three ingredients that must be present—respect, trust, and intimacy. These three cornerstones of the foundation bring the fourth ingredient into being. That fourth element is unity. When we employ the idea of unity or working together for common goals, then we have created the foundation for love.

Love All Things, the Clan Mother of the Seventh Moon Cycle, teaches us that loving relationships revolve around these four elements, creating the circle of these relationships, assuring that the union will stand the tests of time. When we continue to create respect, trust, intimacy, and unity through our devotion to others, and their well-being, we have a foundation that cannot be eroded.

COMPASSION

Compassion has felt the burden
Of a body wracked with pain,
Has wandered on and off the path,
And then returned again.
Compassion has borne the brunt
Of senseless, brutal jests,
And known the fears and agonies
That life presents as tests.
Compassion has been the lonely child,
Crying for comfort in the night,
Facing all the demons alone
And praying for the light.
Compassion has known the struggle
Of healing bitterness and hate,
Refusing to pass the poison on,
Walking through freedom's gate.
Compassion has been the face of
Every human pain and sorrow.
Compassion has held the dream
Of horizons and tomorrow.
Compassion knows no judgment,
Having walked all roads in time,
And praises all weary warriors,
For the mountains they have climbed.

CASUAL CALLOUSNESS
✷

Children played near the racks of drying meat where their mothers worked a short distance away, preparing hides. It was a hot summer day, and the cool river would have been a blessing, but there was much work to be done. The women talked as they worked, but one wasn't talking; she was boasting.

Sings Too Loud always bragged about her family, and her manner irritated the other women. She never thought about how her comments might be seen as making less of others. Her casual callousness tended to create a separation between the women who usually worked together very well, mutually admiring one another's families.

Grandmother Blue Feather was watching from the shade of a cottonwood tree, listening to Sings Too Loud, watching the effect of her callous words on a young mother whose only child had been made fun of by the casual, negative comments. Grandma approached Sings Too Loud, asking her to follow the Old One to the Women's Lodge.

At the lodge, Grandmother Blue Feather's eyes filled with tears as she spoke to Sings Too Loud.

"Don't you see how you are hurting your sisters? You have been callous and unkind. Your words have cut the bonds of the Circle of Sisterhood in two. Why would you work so hard to destroy the love that these women hold for every member of this Tribal family? The Creator gave you a gift, Sings Too Loud, and that gift should be used *to sing the praises* of the goodness you see in everyone. That praise is the love that holds any circle together."

WEDDING SONG

⚏

Sing to me, my husband, of days long gone.
Of nights beneath a melon moon with
Firelight flickering gently and
Love's reflections on the tipi walls.

And I will sing to you, Dreamwalker,
Of sun-filled mornings, the call of doves,
My heart awakening within the protection
Of your strong arms, greeting the day.

And together we will remember the songs
Of those who rode the wind before us,
As they made their way, gathering the goodness
Of the Earth and returning their love to the land.

For we are all that has ever been and
All that ever will be . . .
Reflections of the quest for life or
The spirit within the breeze.

And to that end, our lives are blessed
For we will always be . . .
A part of the Force
That forever exists . . .
Within infinity.

PRODUCT OF LOVE
✄

While the river moved over rounded stones and Nighthawk circled in the twilight, the young mother whispered to the child who suckled at her breast.

"You are the blessing that fell from the stars and took root in my heart, little one. You rested inside my body and I carried you there for nine moons. It gave me joy to carry the burden of such love. I toiled for many hours to give you birth and, finally, the Earth Mother's magnetism drew you into your Earthwalk.

"Now that you are here, I want you to know how my heart sings! The love I bear your father is the stuff of dreams. He has walked the path of strength and has been strong enough to share his dreams with me, as well as his tears. I have entwined my heart with his. He has lent me his courage, he has filled my heart with desire, and he has respected who I am with all that he is. Together, we have walked many trails and have faced each challenge heart-to-heart.

"In you, I see his courage, his determination, his laughing eyes, and his curiosity. In you, I see my gentleness, my compassion, and my desire to live life with joy. There is a love between your parents that fills each day with song, brings a lightness to our steps, and is as enduring as Sacred Mountain. I want you to remember always that you are—and will forever be—a product of that love."

GENTLENESS

Gentleness has melted
Many a hardened heart,
Warming away the numbness,
Giving love a brand new start.

Gentleness brings comfort,
Like a soft summer rain,
Cradling each weary child
From the hunger and the pain.

Gentleness smiles upon
Those who try to meet
Every challenge in the path
Without bowing to defeat.

Gentleness comes to nurture those
Who have forgotten how to sing,
And with loving arms encircles
Their lives with healing dreams.

Gentleness walks a Sacred Path
Tenderly through the years,
Comforting every soul in need,
And through caring, dries their tears.

CONTENTMENT
❈

Contentment comes from an inner serenity that permeates the whole person. The Ancestors spoke of this state of grace and called it Walking in Beauty. When people are at peace with the world, the inner peace that they carry shines, allowing all who see them to recognize their contentment.

In the modern world where accumulating material things seems to be the standard for contentment, we often see that material success does not bring serenity. Many people discover that vanity is not beauty, jewelry does not indicate a person's worth, and haughtiness does not reflect a person's social rank. Contentment comes from being at peace with the Self and with all life, honoring one's connections to the whole without judgments.

Contentment is Cow's Medicine, teaching us to find the joy of being, rather than the joy of having. Where would you find the truth about your personal contentment if you were to make a list of what gives you the joys found in being?

SEARCHING FOR THE OTHER HALF
✂

The human race is always searching for love, belonging, companionship, approval, touch, and genuine caring. These human desires are present in every race, creed, sexual preference, and gender. For any human to embark upon that quest, there must be the desire for union. The mate that will walk with us through all of the up and down cycles of life and will be our trusted companion is often hard to find. My Elders called this special person the other half, or the split-apart.

Every relationship teaches us about ourselves if we have the courage to look within, to see how we can learn from others, and how we can heal the parts of our personalities that struggle against union or unity. In the most personal sense of the word, raw creative energy is released when we come into alignment with our other half, our split-apart. This union grants us the potential to do great things because we learn to trust in the power of love. When we learn to trust ourselves and our mates, divine union is at hand. The lessons may be many, the road may be long, but the human need for union is always eternal. The Great Mystery reminds us that this kind of union is not a lost dream, but is rather a tangible reality. This dream of true love is given as a blessing to those who are willing to seek for their other half, never denying their desire for union, and never losing sight of the heart's goal.

LOVER'S QUEST
✖

Blue thunder, night rain,
With echoes from the pyramids to
Bring me home again.

Within these magic mountains,
A part of me remains,
While another part goes searching
For a lover without a name.

Through misty realms of other dreams
His memory is my quest.
His arms so strong, his heart so bold,
Would bring me to my rest.

And though I hear within my mind
War cries before the ancient flames,
I hear the murmurs of love songs too,
As I sing Dreamwalker's name.

But can it be our paths shall meet,
Only to cross and go on alone?
Or is it that our spirits are bound,
And our hearts, each other's homes.

THE BLESSING OF HUMAN TOUCH

The Great Mystery took the breath of life and blew it into every part of Creation. The spirits of the Two-leggeds, the human beings, were given freewill and intellect so that they could learn about the tangible world in their own unique ways. The Maker of All Things put the Eternal Flame of Love inside the human beings, and that flame created a deep longing in them. This longing for union and for love was coupled with the blessing of human touch, sensuality, sexuality, and all physical sensation.

This gift of love contains the blessings of procreation, physical communication, nurturing, pleasure, and sensual touch. Physical love is a sacred part of being human and carries with it the reflection of Divine Union. To abuse this gift of love is to dishonor the Creator's intent. To sexually shame another, or to misuse one's desire for coupling through force, is to defile the blessing of human touch and union. The Ancient Ones understood that this misuse of sacred, fertile union could bring scarcity and hard times to anyone who broke the guidelines of respect, trust, and intimacy.

LOVES ALL THINGS

Mother, show me how to love
Beyond my human fear;
Teach me all the joys of life
Beyond the veil of tears.

Let me find the pleasure of
A lover's gentle hands;
Let me know the wisdom of
Respect without demands.

Oh, Keeper of Forgiveness,
Teach me how to see
Beyond the petty judgments,
Supporting human dignity.

I will learn your Medicine
Of Mother, lover, friend,
Teaching others how to love
And broken hearts to mend.

Loves All Things, the Clan Mother of the Seventh Moon Cycle, reminds us that love is a many-faceted jewel that gives humans the strength they need to meet the challenges of life. Cherishing one another, and working through all of the barriers we have created that keep us from loving uncondi-tionally, is a lifetime's work. When we show our willingness to stretch and to go to the next level of life's dance with others, we grow. This act of cooperation—the equal desire to grow in unity—is the foundation for un-bridled creation. Desire is the first step of Creation. If we desire and imag-ine a loving environment, we invite it to manifest in our lives.

HEART DRUM
><

When we have made our desire for union known by reclaiming our passion for life, the drums of our hearts call out to others. When we find joy in the commonplace, meeting each day with genuine excitement, others are drawn to us. The gift of a positive point of view is a sure magnet that creates a curiosity in others who want to discover that kind of happiness. The heart drum is playing a melody that cannot be denied when there is a lightness in our steps and a twinkle in our eyes.

The Ancestors called this state of being Walking in Beauty. When a person walks through life in this joyous manner, he or she has found union within the Self and can share that love with others. That person's heart drum will call to others who can recognize the spirit of the happy heart's song.

When we are down, we can change our hearts' sad melody by finding things to admire and appreciate about our lives. By changing our viewpoints to gratitude, we will not draw negative people to us. Our heart drum cannot call sad or miserable souls to us when it is full of praise.

TRUSTED FRIEND

You touched my heart
   and it sang . . .
      of a song long forgotten.

You spoke to me of dreams,
   and I allowed you to know
      a part of me that was painfully shy.

You opened a window to my soul,
   allowing me to be myself,
      and the wind came to cleanse
         my fear of intimacy
            with the fragrance of cedar.

Your walking stick left tracks across
      the trails I follow in my dreams,
And now—
      I am reaching beyond that memory,
         into the distance of future,

Wondering when . . .
      the leaves will change,
         and when you will return.

LANDSCAPE OF THE HEART
✄

The landscape of the heart varies from person to person. Some hearts thrive on conquest, meeting their love of life through the challenges they overcome. The boldness of this kind of heart may contain a landscape fraught with the sheer, granite fronts of mountain peaks, high above the timberline.

Other hearts thrive on gentleness and may reflect a landscape of soft wild flowers, covering a green meadow that slopes to a calm pond. Some hearts paint the picture of wastelands, because life has been a struggle with many burdens to bear. Wild hearts may mirror the passion of a tropical storm or the fiery eruption of volcanoes on an island that represents their independent natures. Passive and bored hearts can sketch a horizon with nothing more than a line to define the difference between earth and colorless sky.

The broken heart is like a shattered mirror, each piece bearing a different picture of some form of lost or unrequited love. This heart represents the unmended suffering of humankind. Every human being feels this kind of fragmentation at one time or another. We encounter this shattering of the heart's landscape when we lose loved ones through death, when we come to the end of a friendship, when we love without having that love returned, when we experience rejection or abandonment of any kind. When we experience this kind of pain, our next step is in learning to heal it.

Loves All Things, the Clan Mother of the Seventh Moon Cycle, reminds us that our personal healing defines our ability to be sensitive in all situations. Once we heal our hurt and anger toward others, we must cross the bridge of forgiving ourselves as well. Has your refusal to forgive the Self or another shattered the landscape of your heart?

SAVAGE PASSION
✖

Buried deep in the heart of every human is a savage, wanton passion for life. To love and to be loved, to go beyond survival and to embrace life to its fullest—these are the primal drives of the heart that allow us to continue, even in the face of all opposition. These feelings have become suppressed in so many humans that the passion of primal, loving instinct has almost come to extinction in many sophisticated nations. Some call this passion animalistic. The Ancestors called it the Force behind Divine Creation. Today's pilgrims on life's road can choose to give it another name—love.

Loves All Things, the Clan Mother of the Seventh Moon Cycle, shows us the pitfalls of losing the wanton, savage passion for life. She reminds us that complacency has replaced our love of life every time we believe that our lives cannot be improved. We forget how many times we have compromised parts of our personal aspirations and dreams. By not loving ourselves enough to keep the dream alive, we have lost trust in our personal abilities, rejecting our tenacity and strength. When our dreams are whittled away, the raw passion of creative force disappears in fragments, mirroring every part of our life dreams that we have denied.

It may be time to love yourself enough to reclaim those lost parts of your dream and to reawaken your savage, wanton passion for life.

THE GIFTED ONES

A person who can take the ordinary and illuminate it, invoking deep feelings in others, is often called a creative genius. The Ancestors call those who carry that talent the Gifted Ones. These are the human beings whose hearts are open to the flow of the inspired mystery of Creation.

Once a person's heart is opened and they discover the wonder of life, the creative flow is available. As long as the heart stays open, it is filled to overflowing, because the constant river of Creation flows through that person's entire being. They can then create from pure joy, and with practice, they can hone their skills to make masterpieces of their lives and anything they choose to create. Some called this state being in love. It is being in love, but not necessarily with another person. It is being in love with the aliveness of being a human being on this wonderful planet, grasping and claiming the potential joy in every act of life.

Is it time for you to open your heart and to fall in love with being human?

PUPPY LOVE
✖

Before a human being becomes cynical, hard-hearted, or lacking feeling, there comes a special, first love. For adults to discount the deep abiding emotions that a young person has for another is criminally insensitive. That hurt can turn a heart cold, causing it to rebel in an unhealthy way.

Yes, it may not be time for the young person to indulge in thoughts of sexuality and marriage, but the well of feelings should be honored. The mistake some parents make is to laugh at puppy love. They may even discount the choice that the young person has made by making ugly remarks about the child's sweetheart. This is damaging and gives the offspring a whole set of new feelings of mistrust.

Loves All Things, Clan Mother of the Seventh Moon Cycle, reminds us that some of the greatest romances found in legends were between passionate adolescents. The sensitivity it takes to handle a situation with delicacy is the adult's responsibility. It is already very painful for young people to grow up in this modern culture without adults using jaded callousness to stamp out heartfelt innocence and loving expression. Is it time for you to remember the special feelings that you encountered during your first love?

PARENTING WITH LOVE

Our parents make the sacrifice
Of providing through the years.
Tending their precious offspring,
Through the joys and the tears.

Being caring and generous,
And then having to be stern,
Giving all the guidelines
Of the lessons to be learned.

The bumps and the illnesses,
The vigils through the night,
Endearing hugs of innocence,
Giving parents such delight.

Then finding the balance,
During the rebellious teens,
By teaching common sense,
Yet allowing them their dreams.

Parenting children with love
Is a test of hopes and fears,
Yet produces a rare treasure
That we can respect and revere.

THE COLD VACUUM OF REJECTION

Any time that one human being forms a bond of caring with another, there are energy lines that connect the two. Seers are aware of these golden filaments that go from one person to another. These lines of energy are connected through the heart and navel areas of the body. Although most people are not aware of the energetic connections, they can be felt as emotions.

When a person cares for another and is rejected, it can be devastating. The energy lines act like a giant rubber band, and when cut at one end, they recoil, slamming into the other person's body. There can be actual physical pain when the energy lines implode into a person's belly. A vacuum is created when the feelings are only present on one side of a relationship.

The examples throughout history of people dying of a broken heart are applicable here. Energy lines have recoiled, wrapping themselves tightly inside the physical body, disallowing the life force to flow. In some instances, the rejection can be healed naturally over time. In other instances, physical illness may follow. In all cases, the healing process requires tenderness and compassion, untangling the life force from the imploded lines of energy. The depth of caring involved determines the rejection's impact and ability to wound.

Knowing this, can we learn to use compassionate communication and sensitivity when we deal with others who care for us, instead of using the cut-and-run tactics that reek of cowardice?

ABUSE OR LOVE?

In matrilineal Native American Tribes, a woman could tear a marriage blanket, leave it outside the lodge with her husband's clothing and hunting gear, and the relationship was over. No questions, no community property, no divorce courts, and no worries about further abuse.

Today, things are more complex. The custody of children, the monetary support, the home, and the fears of not being emotionally supported by friends or family have taken their tolls.

Abuse of any kind, toward any family member, is a common, but unacceptable, illness in our world. The courage to change those situations is found when people love themselves enough to say, "No more!" The fear of future consequences must be balanced with the understanding that unless the pattern of *allowing abuse* is changed, nothing gets healed. The understanding needed is that one's own person (and possibly others) are at risk every time an abuser is allowed to continue the behavior.

Every human being needs to realize that they are worthy of love, dignity, and an abuse-free life. To settle for less is to harbor the feelings of self-rejection, self-hatred, and unrelenting denial. The ability to love the Self is *earned* every time a person makes the decision to break the pattern of abuse.

Are you willing to love yourself enough to say no to abusive behavior toward yourself or at the hands of another?

If your life is abuse free, are you willing to be thankful for that blessing, serving as a healing example of courage for others?

LOVE AND ENDEARMENTS

The preparation for the wedding was underway as all the Tribal Members prepared food for the feast, cleared the Ceremonial Circle, and donned their finest regalia. It was a joyous time because the couple, which would jump the fire together, were loved by everyone.

Finally the time arrived when the couple approached the fire together. The Holy Man smiled as he recognized the love that these two held for one another and for their community. Endearing words of appreciation for the support of their families were spoken by the bride and the groom. Then, each took their turns at speaking to the other, expressing their enduring promises of union. Together, they jumped the fire, bringing the Eternal Flame of Love that dwelt in each together as one.

When he returned to his lodge late that night, the Holy Man reflected on the events of the day. In his pensive mood, one memory kept on returning to his thoughts. No other couple had ever done what this one had done today. They spoke the individual terms of endearment and the usual promises of commitment and devotion. Their eyes had glowed with the love they held for one another. What was it that made this couple seem so different?

Sudden realization came to the Wise One like a flash of desert lightning! This couple pledged the Medicine contained in their love for one another to the community, sharing with all the People the magnitude of their love!

DESIRE FOR A LASTING LOVE
✄

Is there a love so enduring,
It can pass the tests of years?
Is there a heart so forgiving,
It can heal beyond the tears?
Can there be a lover who
Is willing to embrace
The trials and the passion
With an equal grace?

Every heart has these questions,
Every human feels these fears.
Respect, trust, and intimacy,
Wanting a love we can revere.
Will it be a lasting love?
Or will it fade with the years?
That potential lies within us,
If our hearts will persevere.

Every human being is given the opportunity to learn and to grow through relationships. These relationships begin with the self to the Self, then expand to include a mate and family. From there, the circles of relationship grow to include friends, co-workers, all human beings, nature, the planet, and the universe. The key to all these growth processes is found in the willingness to be flexible and grow. Love will last as long as it is tended with unrelenting care. It may grow in a different way from its first intent, but it will grow. How is the Eternal Flame of Love being nurtured in your heart today?

BALANCING OUR SEXUALITY

TO DENY ONE'S SEXUALITY OR TO
BECOME A SLAVE TO ITS PHYSICAL
PLEASURE IS IMBALANCE.

In the Native American way of life, we understand that we are of the Earth. We are given human bodies and eternal spirits so that we can experience the balance between the two.

If all human beings were to deny the drive to procreate, the human species would become extinct. If all humans were to deny the need to be touched, to be hugged, or to be pleasured sexually, we would become hard-hearted robots. On the other hand, if all humans were to become slaves to the physical senses and sexuality, we would never be free enough to discover the unlimited worlds of our infinite spirits.

Discovering the pleasures of physicality and spirituality by bringing both into balance allows humankind to experience heaven and Earth inside of the human form. To love the truth of being human is to see that human beings were created in wholeness and perfection. The Great Mystery did not make any mistakes when humankind was created. If we learn the balancing acts of being human, without judgments, we can have it all.

SEDUCTION OF THE SENSES

Relationships that are based on mutual respect, trust, and intimacy are enduring. All human beings have the potential to find and develop these types of relationships, if they are willing to work through their own shortcomings and allow others to do the same.

In the beginning of any relationship, the use of discernment is necessary. In today's world, many people have learned how to be seducers. To seduce another's senses by saying what one thinks the other wants to hear is an act of dishonesty. To behave one way in order to attain another's trust, while denying one's true intent or nature, is an act of cowardice. The labels human beings have affixed to these behaviors are social climber, gold digger, user, seducer, yesman, home wrecker, scam artist, gigolo, groupie, and so forth. These tragic misuses of human potential defy explanation. The ultimate lessons of allowing ourselves to be seduced by our senses, or our longings to be accepted, admired, or loved, are often very painful.

Honesty in all relationships begins within. If we are loving toward ourselves, using self-respect, self-trust, and honest intimacy, by examining our intents, discerning these traits (or the lack of these traits) in others becomes an easy task.

Is it time to examine whether you have ever been seduced or have been a seducer through your lack of honesty with the Self?

8TH
MOON

YOU CAN HEAL

There is nothing that has been done to you or that you have done to yourself that the Great Mystery and the Earth Mother cannot heal.

She Who Heals is the Clan Mother of the Healing Arts, who teaches us about the miracles of healing. There is a force greater than our human understanding that suggests that the desire to live and to heal is more powerful than any medication, operation, or healing art. To give up is to forget one's connection to the Creator and the Earth Mother, as well as this promise of healing that was given to all living things.

HEALING MISSION
✖

Before the Two-leggeds and the Creature-beings arrived on the planet, the Earth Mother decreed that there would be no illness or disease among the ones with physical bodies that could not be healed. The power of healing any illnesses was given to the Plant People.

The creatures were given instinct so that they would know which plants were going to heal them when they felt unfit. The Human Tribe was told to watch the Creature-teachers in order to learn from them. The human beings learned for a while, and then, in arrogance, they adopted the idea that they were superior to the other creatures.

The Earth Mother frowned, because the further away from the natural world her human children strayed, the more illness they brought upon themselves. Finally, they had infected All Their Relations. The Earth Mother cleansed the natural world by freezing all the sickness and started over.

Those who survived had heard the Mother's voice and were willing to respect their plant and creature Relations. To this day, the Human Tribe is still looking for the pieces of the lost healing knowledge held by the Plant Tribe. The Earth Mother and the Great Mystery have promised that those cures are still there, awaiting rediscovery. They have also promised to freeze the Earth again—if we fail in our missions to heal that which we have made sick or if we fail to clean the parts of our world we have harmed.

THE ROLE OF HEALING
✖

There are many unseen factors present when a person asks for a healing. Some people feel they need to keep their illness in order to receive love. In order to give love, others may need to have the role of taking care of an invalid.

A healer or Medicine Person is only a conduit for healing. The Medicine Person has to put aside any personal need to be successful, coming from a pure heart and allowing the Great Mystery to do the actual work. The desire of the sick person to get well has to be present, along with that person's willingness to let go of whatever created the illness. The sick person must trust that the Creator can work through the Medicine Person, letting go of hopelessness, thereby being willing to receive the healing.

No healing is ever a failure. The only failure is in giving a healing to boost one's self-importance or in refusing to receive healing in order to punish the Self or another.

GATHERING HERBS

To gather the healing herbs that would be used in her remedies, a Medicine Woman would rise before dawn and do her morning prayers, giving thanks for the day. When the first rays of sunlight touched the plants, she would go to the largest plant of that variety, asking permission to take only what she needed. That Chief Plant could give or deny permission by speaking to the woman's heart. If permission was granted, she would pass the first seven plants without taking anything, in order to leave enough for the next seven generations.

At each plant she approached, she would ask for that plant to give of its healing power. If the request was denied, she would move to another plant, only gathering those that were willing to give of their life force to help her make healing herbal remedies. At that early hour, while the dew was still present, the life force of the plant was at its height. To gather later, in the heat of the day, would mean less life force for her remedies.

The Medicine Woman's respect of the Plant Tribe, and the plant's willingness to assist humankind, allows us to see why those remedies carried strong Medicine. Working with the unified flow of all things in the natural world is one way that humankind can access more potent solutions—reverently, taking and using less.

WOUNDED SPIRITS

Oh, you of wounded spirits,
I offer you a place of rest;
Walk among my mountains,
And climb to Eagle's nest.
Come swim amid my oceans,
Or feel my desert's fire.
Sit beside running waters
To reclaim your heart's desire.
Seek my silent forests,
Or walk my open plains,
Travel the deepest jungles
'Til you hear my love's refrain.
I am always waiting
To allow each child to heal,
To cradle the wounded spirits,
And teach them how to feel.
I am the Earth Mother,
Who loves without regret,
Tending all my children,
Who through tears
    have paid all debts.

DEATH WISH

The bitter young woman could take the jealousy that ate her spirit no more. She had hurt the ones she loved. She carried a burden of guilt and shame that weighted every step. She had spit her hatred into the world, and now, friendless and alone, she cried out to the Great Mystery.

"Great and Eternal Mystery, I ask that I may die to the ways of hate and be reborn in love. I ask that this hateful burden be lifted and that my eyes be healed. I have chosen to see wickedness in every person around me. I have looked without seeing, taken without giving, blamed without reason, and shamed others without regret. The poison within me has hardened my heart and numbed my senses. I cannot do it alone, please help me!"

The Creator sent the Earth Mother to help the woman who sobbed, crying out in her pain. The Earth Mother whispered to her erring daughter, and through the tears the woman heard.

"Daughter, this is not the end; it is the beginning. Your heart is on the mend because you have recognized the folly of your ways. You are free now to die a little each day, giving away your pain and sorrow. You are also free to be reborn into the love that has always been available. Your burden has been heavy, but now you are home. Forgiving yourself, and learning to give caring back to those you have hurt, is the way to heal. Come cradle in my arms, and I will give you rest."

HEALING THE POISONS

Throughout time, as human beings, we have poisoned our hearts with bitterness. We have poisoned our thoughts with jealousy and greed. We have poisoned our bodies with unhealthy foods and artificial substances. We have poisoned our spirits with our lack of gratitude. In this sickened state, the human race has lost sight of what this crooked trail has done to the world around us.

We have dumped chemicals into the waters, buried the toxins in the soil, poisoning the Earth, the creatures, and the Plant People. Many humans feel helpless to stop the ravaging that is taking place on the Earth Mother. To find the solutions, we must begin at home by being conscious of how we can contribute to the answers and the clean up. We are being asked to recycle, to reuse, and to be conscious of our consumption.

On a personal level, we are being asked to clean up and heal our thoughts, our emotions, our intentions, our old pain, our denials, our physical health, and our actions. When we become personally responsible for the healing of every thought, action, intention, and deed in our lives, the rest of the world will heal along with us.

Are you ready? Get out the scouring powder and decide which kinds of poisons in your life you would like to start on first.

THE PURPOSE OF MOURNING

When a loved one dies, we mourn our losses. In many cultures, people are taught to grieve with near-silent tears because it is unseemly to fall apart. In other cultures, professional mourners are hired by families to wail, cry, and tear their hair to assist the bereaved family members in accessing and releasing their deepest griefs.

Among Indian People, there have been many forms of mourning: cutting one's hair off, blackening one's face with soot, or going alone to a solitary place and making cuts on the ankles and forearms to allow the blood to flow into the Earth Mother. In some Tribes, the ancient custom was to burn all possessions of the deceased, never speaking the person's name again, so that the loved one's spirit would not be drawn back to the physical world.

In all cases, the Red Race taught the mourners to wail and cry out their pain and sorrow. The purpose of mourning was to empty the burden of grief from the bodies of those who remained behind. Our Wise Ancestors understood that grieving was a part of the healing process. Talking about sorrow can impound the burden. To shed the tears, and wail out all the feelings, is to free the mourner from what is in the past. The mourner and the spirit of the one who has Dropped the Robe are both free to go on to the next step on the Wheel of Life.

She Who Heals reminds us that if we are stuck in memories of the past, we can heal through grieving and releasing these sorrows. Then, we are ready to face our lives, being present and aware of the Now.

RELEASING THE SPIRIT
✂

It is the custom among many Traditional Natives to release the spirit of any creature who has died. This custom was originally used to thank the animals who provided food for the families of hunters. The hunter would show respect for the life of that creature, and return thanks for the sacrifice the creature made, apologizing for taking its life. An offering of tobacco, corn pollen, or cornmeal would accompany a prayer of gratitude and releasing that would allow that creature's spirit to return to the Creator.

Among our Traditional People, this ceremony is still done today, showing deep respect for any creature's life. Respect is shown whether the death occurred during hunting or if the animal is a "roadkill." When any creature is hit by a car or dies by flying into a power line, the respect for that life is shown by acknowledging the role it held in the family of All Our Relations. To release the spirits of our creature Relations is to recognize that without our creature cousins, life would not be complete. These spirits can then continue by going on to their next step on the Medicine Wheel of Life.

When we show gratitude toward all living things, and for the roles they hold in Creation, we acknowledge their purposes. We also honor our roles as Guardians and caretakers. As Guardians, we acknowledge the completion of that life form's cycle on the Medicine Wheel, allowing a new cycle to be born.

HEALING PRAYER

Mother, teach me how to heal
The feelings inside of me;
Teach me how to respect all life
With burgeoning humility.

Show me the path away from abuse,
Where everything sings of life,
Where heartache is just a memory
Of ancient, human strife.

Let my spirit be healed
Until dying holds no fear,
Where rebirth is welcomed,
Bringing me joyous tears.

These are the things that I desire,
For I want to truly know,
The pathways and healing passage
Through the dark night of the soul.

HEALING AND PATIENCE
✂

Patience is a quality that is necessary in order to have any kind of healing take place. We are taught to rush about in our modern lives and to accomplish as much as possible in a day. Yet, when it comes to the body, we cannot hurry the healing process. The body repairs itself at its own rate. Babies are born in their own time. Cuts and broken bones mend when the body is strong enough to produce new cells, and there is no way a human being can force the body to mend faster.

In Native American culture, we honor any person who has patience. We see the quality of patience as a teacher that shows us how to slow down. The calmness that people employ in their day-to-day lives is a sure sign of balance. When a person has to be talking, hurrying, fidgeting, or actively engaged all the time, this reflects that person's agitation with life. This constant agitation shows the astute observer that the person has not come to a place of healing. Physical, mental, emotional, and spiritual healing cannot take place without patience and stillness.

HEALING HEARTACHE
✂

I looked to find my heart was breaking;
I could not stop the pain,
   Not then,
      or now.
In the place where trust had been,
   Betrayal stood . . . alone . . . the victor.
      My tears would have filled an ocean . . .
         Had I had the strength to cry.

Privacy appears on my doorstep
         with the night,
   And with the night comes my loneliness
         and my fear.

The Earth Mother's love has made me stronger,
         so tonight I will let the hills hold me . . .
            and my company will be the wind.

HEALING FRUSTRATION
✖

When frustration and anxiety overwhelm our sense of well-being, it is time to take a break. Nothing can be done about the confusion or the lack of clarity when we are in the same environment that created the situation. When everything we touch or try to do ends up falling short, we are out of sync with our body's rhythms, the Thought World, and the rhythms of the Earth Mother that allow our lives to flow with ease.

Healing this type of frustration is accomplished by stopping all activity. That is to say that we can change the chaos, allowing the ease of desired manifestation, by changing our internal rhythms. Taking a walk and breathing deeply, calming the senses, and noticing things that we can admire about the outdoors can shift our perceptions. When we feel the new rhythm of calmness flow through our bodies, we will then be stepping into a new point of view, allowing clarity to come. When we see the clear picture of what we want and intend, we ask the Earth Mother to bless that idea or mental picture by manifesting it in the tangible world. When we show our gratitude for new clarity and the manifestation of our ideas, we have completed the circle between the Thought World and the Natural World. We have then healed our frustration by being in sync with both worlds, and we *become* the connection that brings the two worlds together as one. From this point of balance, all things become possible and we can create at will.

PERSONAL DEATH AND REBIRTH CYCLES
✂

When we look at life cycles, we see fertility, death, and rebirth in all things. All human beings go through many endings and many beginnings in their lifetimes. These life cycles carry deaths that are merely changes in how a person operates in the sphere of the tangible world. The changes or deaths can be labeled divorce, job change, new address, or birthday.

Every person starts a death cycle fifty-eight days—two twenty-eight-day moon cycles plus two new moon days—prior to a birthday, marking a Rite of Passage that consists of reviewing the events and lessons of the prior year and then letting go of the past. For some, this process comes in the form of sadness or stress. Most human beings do not know that they are in their personal death cycle. Many come to resent the anniversary of the day of their birth, forgetting that they are beginning a rebirth cycle at the sun's dawning on the day of their birth.

The opportunities for growth and further development hold special promise if people are willing to let go of any judgment they have held regarding their past. These regrets have no place in the rebirth cycle and must be laid to rest, along with any self-rejection or personal criticism. Being authentically aware of the new opportunities placed in our paths requires some work.

This Rite of Passage calls for acceptance of what has gone before, forgiveness of others and the Self, and a determination to embrace the new with a happy heart. In this manner, all human beings can begin again without regret, allowing the mystery of life to unfold in their lives.

SHE WHO HEALS
✖

Mother, sing me a song
That will ease my pain,
Mend broken bones,
Bring wholeness again.

Catch my babies
When they are born,
Sing my death song,
Teach me how to mourn.

Show me the Medicine
Of the healing herbs,
The value of spirit,
The way I can serve.

Mother, heal my heart
So that I can see
The gifts of yours
That can live through me.

She Who Heals, the Clan Mother of the Eighth Moon Cycle, shows humankind that every act of life is a cycle or step on the path to healing. When we learn how to let go of our need to hold on to the past, we heal our formerly limited potential for growth. When we find courage and faith inside ourselves, we can heal our fear of future. When we refuse to mentally degrade ourselves or another, the mind clears and allows us to be present—conscious of everything that is happening in the moment. These are all examples of healing the fragments of our lives that need to come into wholeness. When we go beyond the places where we have become numb, we feel life again. When we learn to feel again, we can heal.

RED NATIONS' HEALING PROCESS
✖

There is a valuable secret to healing that is held by the Red Race. The Native American people are going through a healing crisis in these modern times. We are reawakening to what we have always known: The sacred mountains are our foundations, the rivers run through our veins, the trees are our backbones, and the creatures are our teachers. These understandings give us the strength to heal our hearts and our spirits of two hundred years of shame.

We are learning how to heal addictions through the wisdom of our Ancestors' ways. We are nurturing the seeds of cooperation and sharing that were blown away by the winds of adopting the worst of the white man's ways. And now we are being asked to heal the lies and separation that have taken hold inside our own communities.

Divide and conquer was an idea brought from Europe that took Native America by surprise. This idea cut the Circles that contained our sense of wholeness. Today, we, like all other races, are learning how to heal the splits within ourselves. We are asking for guidance, and many are finding that we can no longer continue the ideas of separation if we are to heal. We are at the same crossroad as all other nations on this Earth. We must decide to embrace the healing found in unity that makes us spiritually strong.

Is today the time for you to let go of the ideas that keep you from seeing all humans as family?

THE SECRET OF LIFE FORCE

Human beings can survive on very little to eat and drink. They can continue to exist even if they are worked beyond reason. Humankind can live without education or understanding, religion or spirituality, in ignorance of politics and world events. Human beings can endure pain and suffering, disappointment and heartache, and the loss of material comforts. But, humans will wither, become ill, and die if they are not loved and cherished as family.

She Who Heals, the Clan Mother of the Eighth Moon Cycle, reminds us that nobody can live without love.

Is it time to drop the places where you isolate yourself, forgetting to reach out to those you trust when you are down?

It may be time to show others whom you may have forgotten that you do cherish them by spending some quality time together.

All humans' life force is strengthened when they are demonstratively *shown that they are loved. Is it time for you to give or to receive a hug?*

HEALING THE WILL
✖

The heart of every human holds
The feelings and the dreams
Of deepest aspirations,
Freewill's creative esteem.
The urge toward higher purpose,
The drive to create from grace,
Unlimited power of expression,
The potential of the human race.
Yet, the side roads are many,
Blighted by denial and fear,
Refusal to express the feelings,
Until numbness blocks our tears.
Lost in our machinations,
Yet craving release from pain,
Surrender may not come sweetly,
But the will can be regained.
The sacredness of being lies
In feeling all that appears,
Without applying judgments
To the joys or to the fears.
Trusting every emotion as
Something we created to feel,
Then expressing every feeling,
Allows the will to heal.

HEALING HUMILIATION

HUMILIATION IS THE ONE EVENT IN HUMAN LIFE
THAT BECOMES UNFORGETTABLE. THE LOSS OF HUMAN
DIGNITY AT THE HANDS OF ANOTHER CAN BE
FORGIVEN, BUT IT IS RARELY, IF EVER, FORGOTTEN.

Healing humiliation and loss of human dignity is something that comes from inside a person. No healer, psychologist, doctor, Medicine Person, or teacher can do it for another. Consciously shaming another has dealt many a blow throughout time. Kicking people when they are vulnerable is a tactic of insensitive bullies. The world has been fraught with this behavior since its inception.

It never seems to happen when we are feeling strong. It most always happens when we are dealing with our own self-doubt and self-criticism. We can heal the need to experience this reflection, coming from the Great Smoking Mirror, which our inner thoughts project for us to see. The key is to notice that if we stop beating ourselves up internally, the bullies in the world don't pick on us. The lesson of losing our dignity through being humiliated is learned when we show mercy toward ourselves. Deciding that we have a right *to be,* supporting that right with kindness, instead of judgments, may not make us forget the incident, but it will allow us to forgive ourselves. Forgiving others by thanking them for showing us what we were doing to ourselves internally allows us to see the opportunity to change our mental patterns and heal.

HEARTSTRINGS, THE THREADS OF LIFE

When Wood Song was captured by the brutal warriors of another Tribe, she trusted her family to find her. The nightmarish days dragged into moons as she was marched southward on little water or food. The beatings and forced march were wearing her body out. The cold nights without the comfort of a blanket chilled more than her body.

Finally, Wood Song came to a place where the hope of rescue died, numbing her senses and killing her desire to live. Each day after that, she cut one more heartstring that kept her tied to life. Her heart's threads became frazzled and frayed by the loss of hope and constant abuse. She knew that those too ill to continue were left to die.

One morning, Wood Song's fragile body was released from the hemp knots that tied her to the hostage in front of her and rolled down a rocky, cactus-covered embankment. The vultures circled, and her lips bled from lack of water. The weakened heartstrings broke, one after another, leaving her on the brink of death.

Wood Song was about to cut the last heartstring to her family with the thought that they had not loved her because she was just a girl child, when a shadow crossed her face. Something splashed on her lips; it was salty. Opening her eyes, she saw the tears spilling from her big brother's face. Loving arms encircled her, and the threads of life were restored. She would survive and heal. She would go home. She knew that she was loved. The heart hardened by abuse was gone, being replaced with her Medicine, the healing song of the forests, played on heartstrings of love.

THE PERSONAL CREED
※

There is a valuable healing tool that can assist all human beings in making the most of their lives. This tool allows us to live by our own volition and with our own integrity. This tool is the personal creed. The values that each individual wants to live by are not immutable. When we see that something needs updating, we simply do it. A personal creed can give us focus and allow us to see life as a healing process because it does not focus on *don'ts*.

We can see how a personal creed could be of assistance through the following example:

> *To the best of my ability—*
> I intend to respect all life. I choose to be account-
> able for my decisions. I intend to support Elders
> and children with my time, my resources, and my
> caring. I choose not to judge myself or others. I
> choose to speak the truth in all situations. I
> choose to learn from my mistakes and shortcom-
> ings. I choose not to revile or to abuse myself with
> criticism or to reject my human growth process.

If living with a personal guideline that affirms your integrity appeals to you, it may be time to make a personal creed that you feel good about. The result could allow you to gain added focus and integrity, supporting the way you choose to live your life.

THE AFTERMATH OF BATTLE

In the aftermath of battle,
When cruelty has counted coup,
And weary hearts are broken,
And wounds need seeing to,
There comes a song of mourning,
That sings of things that died,
The loss of innocence and of trust,
Killing human dignity and pride.
Abuse and shame, used as spears,
Can wound every human soul;
In the aftermath of this battle,
We see the countless human tolls.
The malady of human cruelty,
And what it has done to us all,
Is reason enough for inventing
Human illness and numbing walls.
The final battle of each spirit
Is in finding the courage to heal,
Facing the future with bravery,
Banishing abuse, while learning to feel.
Each tangle with these shadows
Yields a fragment of the whole,
Until we can count the victory
Over the dark night of the soul.

THE MALADY OF INDIFFERENCE

In a world where we have been blasted by every kind of sensory perception, stimulus pollution has taken its toll. Many people have lost the sense of what disturbs them, due to these horrors being a common occurrence. More and more frequently, we defer, as a society, to the ravages of crime, domestic abuse, and insensitivity. We must realize that locking our doors, ignoring these terrors that besiege the senses, does not stop the intrusions.

The malady of indifference and apathy has forced some to turn away, while others build an excess of emotional armor that tends to turn their hearts cold. The fear is masked by those who are affluent through the use of security systems and only traveling in "the better neighborhoods."

Changes take place when healing solutions are carried out by concerned citizens. Having cast off the masks of indifference, these courageous individuals seek to better the conditions for every neighborhood. Volunteering to make a difference in a young person's life offers alternative paths for our youth. By using our time today to guide young minds and personalities, we are healing our own indifference. Assuring the adults of tomorrow that we care enough to rehabilitate our own sensitivity and caring, dropping the armor of jaded senses and changing our indifference to—making a difference.

RENEWAL THROUGH THE DREAMTIME
✄

In many cultures, out-of-body journeying is used to bring renewal to a person's sense of well-being. When journeying, all stress is removed from the physical body, the mind, the emotions, and the spirit. The letting go of earthly concerns that allows the spirit to travel is a learned skill. When the traveling spirit returns to the body, the energy in the body shifts again, bringing renewal to the entire human organism.

When a human being experiences body death, the same journey is accomplished without the need to return to the physical vehicle. Some people believe that their spirits go to heaven, nirvana, the Spirit World, or paradise. All of these concepts are individual ways of labeling what my Elders called Dreamtime. The nontangible world, where all is pure energy, exists as a parallel to our tangible world. The membrane that separates these worlds is very thin and can be accessed with practice.

Elderly people, who go in and out of remembering who and where they are, do not have to practice. Their spirits choose to journey effortlessly because their bodies are worn out, not holding on to the need to be in tangible reality. This is a beautiful Dreamtime state, which should not be judged as bad because it enables the Elders to experience crossing over without fear. When this journey occurs, spiritual renewal, through letting go of a worn-out body, is at hand.

UNQUESTIONING FAITH

THE INNOCENCE OF UNQUESTIONING FAITH HAS
INSTIGATED MANY A MIRACULOUS CURE, BEFUDDLING
SOME OF THE MOST VALUED SCIENTIFIC MINDS.
HOW CAN ANY HUMAN BEING REFUSE TO BELIEVE
IN MIRACLE HEALING WHEN PRESENTED WITH
ABSOLUTE PHYSICAL EVIDENCE?

There is no way to present to science the repeatability needed to establish test results when, against all odds, a miraculous cure has happened. In the cases where unquestioning faith has removed a mountain of tumors in a matter of a few days, I have actually heard angry comments from the medical community directed at the healed individual. *What is wrong with this picture?*

Aren't we supposed to want everyone to be well? Does it matter how it happens? Can we afford to limit our human resources by insisting that healing can only occur through one specialized avenue or group of people?

She Who Heals, the Clan Mother of the Eighth Moon Cycle, reminds us that self-importance blocks us from ever attaining unquestioning faith. Without self-importance, people can acquire the faith of knowing that their gifts will be used for the highest good, when the time is right. The goal of having a healed world can then be accessed through cooperation, but never through competition. If your need to be acknowledged has kept you from sharing something that could be of value, ask yourself: Do I have the courage to heal by embracing unquestioning faith and become a part of the answer? Or does my ego fear that I will never be acknowledged for contributing to the answer?

INTUITION'S LEGACY
‡

*There is a place inside us
Where we feel what we know.
If we act on that intuition,
Doors open, urging us to grow.
The legacy of inner knowing
Comes from Great Mystery's grace;
Learning to trust these feelings
Is a talent we develop and embrace.
Ultimate trust of the Self,
And inspiration's guiding light,
Allows humankind to develop
The rare gifts of second sight.
When we embrace growth potential,
Feeling—with all that we are—
Then the legacy of intuition
Allows us to reach for the stars.
Nothing outreaches our senses,
Nothing is too hard to attain,
We serve the truth through healing
The limitations our minds contain.
Intuition is born from reflecting
All the senses that we can feel,
Then implicitly trusting that knowing
Gives the guidance that allows us to heal.*

HEALING OUR DEFENSE MECHANISMS
✄

Timber Bear was always complaining about the way he never seemed to be able to find a woman who wanted to be his mate, showing the observer his feelings of inadequacy. At other times, he was known to expound upon the multitude of needed requirements of any woman who would have the *honor* of being his wife, revealing his puffed-up, yet fragile, sense of self-importance.

One day Timber Bear's wise father took him aside and had a talk with his confused son. He told Timber Bear that his loneliness was self-created. His father explained that women avoid men who refuse to see the inner beauty in other people, seeing only the physical body or social graces. The man who looks for ultimate perfection in a woman shows the world that he is deeply wounded, having no real sense of who he is as a man. If a man knows who he is, and what he is about, he can acknowledge his strengths and his faults with equal humility. When a man has healed his insecurities, there is no need to have *the perfect woman* to fill in what he feels is lacking in himself. He can love others for who they are—not for how they look or what they do.

Timber Bear's father waited for his words to sink in, then he spoke from his heart. "My son, all human beings use any method they can to defend the hurt places inside themselves, but it is the use of those same defenses that keep people from healing. You cannot shoot arrows into the world through your words and attitudes without hitting other wounded people who will equally defend their hurts with arrows of their own."

HEALING OUR IMMUNE SYSTEMS
✂

To heal the immune systems of the Earth Mother, we need a concerted effort to clean the pollution and toxic waste on our planet. To heal the immune systems of the animal kingdom, we need to stop putting poisons in the foods they eat or injecting them with unnatural substances. To heal the human immune system is a bit more involved because we have several kinds of immune systems.

The strength of the physical immune system is dependent on the what we consume in the way of air, water, other liquids, medications, and food. These clean-up jobs can be accomplished through personal determination. Due to various new diseases, the decisions to care about our health also include prevention and our willingness to avoid known risks.

The emotional immune system is different. We are not immune to abusive behavior, and emotional or verbal attack. The continuance of being the recipient of this ugly behavior affects people's overall immune system. When people believe they have no way out, the seeming lack of choices has put *the will* (emotional body) in denial. Mental or physical illness will follow when the emotional immune system is overloaded with denied feelings and refused freewill.

Have you put your health at risk by denying your feelings or your right to make choices about what you are willing to experience or consume? Healing note: *Digesting emotional toxins can cause chronic indigestion of the spirit and a lack of immunity to feeling helplessness and hopelessness.*

9TH
MOON

PLACE OF THE SETTING SUN

Each setting sun marks a Rite of Passage. This is the time when day passes the Sacred Pipe to the night. The twilight marks a sudden stillness that shows Mother Nature holding her breath, waiting to exhale the Sacred Pipe's smoke. The hushed silence signals the time for each of us to return thanks for the things we have been able to accomplish, the opportunities we have grasped, and the lessons we have learned.

As the daylight dies, we are reminded that we are approaching a time of rest. To sleep, to dream, to collect our vital life force. When we pass through the night, we have crossed over an invisible canyon that echoes the Earth Mother's loving desire for our continued growth. Her whispers are carried on the backs of Wind Spirits; they permeate our dreams.

Her voice calls to our spirits, "Children of Earth, you have grown during this passing Sun. You have successfully moved through this day's Rite of Passage. Rejoice! And may you never be the same again."

PLACE OF TOMORROW
⋈

Placing untold value on the needs of the next Seven Generations is the way of the wise. Preparing for tomorrow's needs insures the continuance of life abundant. Returning thanks to the Ancestors who knew these things shows gratitude for the blessings that were shared by those who came before us, taking only what they needed. Those Ancestors protected the Earth's resources in order to assure that there would be enough to provide for your family today.

Setting Sun Woman, the Clan Mother of the Ninth Moon Cycle, teaches us the value of conservation and reminds us to share what we have with those who are in need. She asks us to be mindful of how we can serve the other Children of Earth.

Is it time to volunteer some of your time, or share some of your food, or recycle some clothing you no longer wear?

Where can you conserve energy? Where can you use less and recycle more?

How much are you committed to the survival of every living thing? Can you embrace the truth of your answers? If not, it may be time for a change.

ASSUMPTIONS ABOUT TOMORROW
✄

The little mushrooms were pushing through the mosses in the undergrowth, signaling that the autumn rains were bringing the time of gathering. Two Clouds was teaching the young women of her Clan how to know which kinds of mushrooms were edible, and how to collect them.

One young woman was filling her basket with every edible mushroom she could find. Two Clouds noticed and stopped the women, asking them to form a circle so they could talk. Then Two Clouds began her lesson.

"We can never assume what tomorrow will bring for our children and their children. If we take all the mushrooms we see, there will be none left to continue the generations of food that can be foraged from the forest. We might discover that our great grandchildren died of hunger because we took unfair advantage of the bounty given to us today.

"There is a balance in the natural world that we can sense, but we cannot always see. If the buffalo keep disappearing, and the deer and the flocks of winged creatures change their migration patterns, how will our generation survive? In assuming that there will always be more than enough, we have forgotten that we are ultimately responsible for what tomorrow holds. If we take without giving something back, we have robbed tomorrow of the energy it needs for renewal."

A PROMISE OF TOMORROW

The promise Creator gives us
Comes with every new day,
The gift of breath, the gift of life,
Opportunities in a vast array.
How do we count our blessings,
Through the choices life can bring?
Is it through joyful lessons?
Or the fears to which we cling?
Are we learning to show gratitude,
For the victories over human pain?
By honoring the feeling choices,
We grasp the will we've regained.
Can we change our focus,
With no need to defend?
Acknowledging joy and sorrow,
Without judging foe or friend?
Tomorrow promises the fullness
Of every human way to know;
How we master each challenge
Determines our balance—
   reflecting how we grow.

INDIAN GIVING
><

The concept of Indian Giving has been misunderstood for a long time. Our Native American Ancestors taught us that every living thing and inanimate object in our world has a mission. Whether it be a sweater, a cook pot, a lodge, a stone, or a tree. When a gift is given to another, the person receiving that gift must understand the gift's mission. The use of the object given determines its purpose. If the recipient does not use the gift, the purpose and mission of service contained in that object is dishonored.

When this occurs, the giver has the right to reclaim the gift, giving it to another person who needs it or will use it. Then the usefulness of the object will serve its purpose and be able to complete its mission.

If a person has many blankets and another person has none, it is perfectly all right to take the unused blanket back and give it to someone who needs it. In this way, the blanket's gift, of bringing warmth, is honored as having been useful to humankind.

Setting Sun Woman, the Clan Mother of the Ninth Moon Cycle, teaches us that if we are not using something and others are in need, it is time to pass it on so that the usefulness of the object can be honored. One way we can prepare for tomorrow is by making sure that we never waste the usefulness of anything that is needed today.

THE VALUE OF MEMORIES
✖

The precious moments linger,
The warmness still remains,
Old friends and fond memories,
A shelter from the rain.
The richness of memories
Invites laughter to return,
Banishing the stormy skies,
Petty problems, and concerns.
Reach deep within your memory,
To a shining moment in time,
Retrieving every sentiment,
To reclaim the sublime.
The value of our memories
Is a store of wealth untold,
A smile on a cloudy day,
And a fire to feed the soul.

Setting Sun Woman, the Clan Mother of the Ninth Moon Cycle, teaches us that dwelling on difficulties can weaken our problem-solving abilities. Sometimes we need to shift gears, to recall happy times, or to take a walk before we return to the challenges in our paths. The value of fond memories is found when we use the simple technique of focusing on something that gave us joy. The mental gears switch from effort to relaxation. Then we can find balance, feeling refreshed and having a new approach to our challenges.

RESPONDING TO NEEDS

In ancient times, among Native American People, some of the rules of etiquette regarding responsibility to others were

> Never look into another person's lodge when passing by—respect that family's privacy.
>
> Never touch another's belongings without permission—not even a child's possessions.
>
> Never let the children, Elders, the sick, or the infirm go without food or care.
>
> Never withdraw your allegiance given to another, especially in times of need.
>
> Never forget the acts of kindness and support that were granted when you were in need.
>
> Take action when a crisis situation warrants your response. Act in silence unless directing others is necessary. Less talk prevents chaos.
>
> Never do anything that would hurt the Children, Elders, or Life Givers (women).
>
> Never offer advice unless it is asked for by another. Unwanted assistance can defeat another's purpose and determination to do for the Self.
>
> Always ask what is needed, and then listen to the answer. Give of the Self and be generous with your material gifts. When giving, always be mindful of the recipient's dignity and ability to receive.

These simple rules of thumb are considered proper responses to the needs of others—being respectful, generous, kind, honest, and willing to take action in times of trouble.

LIGHTNING GLASS

The young man walked the desert with his father, hunting for the tracks that could bring food to the family. The younger warrior stopped, picked something up, and held it up to the sun. His face was bent into a curious expression when his father turned to see him. Silently, the young one walked to his father and, holding out the object, shrugged without speaking. The father smiled a big smile and took his son into the shade of a nearby mesquite tree. In order not to scare any nearby game, the younger warrior had been careful not to speak. In reverent whispers his father explained.

"This is the mark of the Fire-sticks. When the Sky Father makes love to the Earth Mother, the bolts of fire hit the sands of her body, making this red glass. It is a symbol of their love and of the faith they share for all tomorrows. To find this rare drop of the Earth Mother's blood is a good thing. It carries the Medicine of the Thunder Bird along with the promise of the Earth Mother to bring you a mate who will match your wisdom and your Medicine. The passion and love between you two will equal the love that the Sky Father has for the Earth Mother."

PROMISE OF TOMORROW

The promise of tomorrow
Depends upon the way
We honor all the blessings
That are ours today.
Can we hear the voices of
The children yet unborn?
Do they call to us with gratitude,
Or do we hear their scorn?
Are we so wrapped up in taking
That we forget to give?
Wasting every resource that
Allows the future to live.
Have we killed the promise
Of tomorrows yet to be?
Or will we stop the plunder
Of our greed's insanity?
The children of the future,
Sing out in the night.
Their song asks for mercy,
A release from their plight.
We can make a difference,
We can show we care,
By honoring all the blessings
Of fire, water, earth, and air.

FIGHTING FOR LIFE

✂

> IF WE DO NOT FIGHT FOR LIFE,
> WE WILL NEVER COUNT THE COUP
> OF LIVING WELL.

Fighting for life is not through violence. Today, we are asked to fight for life through the way of the peaceful warrior. The way to claim our personal rights of living well is by walking through life as peace-makers, turning away from malice, revenge, bitterness, envy, hatred, and negativity. When these traits are not present, we can naturally celebrate our lives with joy.

The soldier of bygone days stood at the edge of his circle and faced the threatening forces outside. Today, the peaceful warrior still stands at the edge of his or her circle, turning with courage to face the enemy within. We fight for life when we are willing to confront, and to heal, our personal issues. We are then counting the victory coup on the internal negative forces that can keep us from living well.

AUTUMN DAWN
✂

The earliest pink of dawn crept across the Valley of Miracles. I lit a fire to greet the Dawn Star. The flames sang out and met the colors of fiery leaves, merging in the first rays of sunlight, uniting the red scrub oaks that walled the canyons with the magical valley below.

Although I could not see his face, Grandfather Sun's rays peaked above the eastern slopes, setting the western ridge on fire with the warmth of his light. The starlings began their dance of life, coming from their mud nests high in the cliff face, looking across the singing waters of Golden Earth Creek.

Four and a half million years ago, the glacier had made this valley, followed by the melting ice that cut snakelike ribbons through the Earth Mother's body, creating the creek bed, giving the Water Spirits a home. I became the witness to the wonder of all that had gone before. There, in my silence, listening to the songs of nature, my heart cried out, "Life is good!" As if they heard my silent scream, the Raven cawed, the Eagle flew over, the fire crackled, and we were one.

ACCEPTING WHAT IS OFFERED

When a Native American offers a gift or a meal, it is very rude not to accept what is being offered. A Native American person may not have much material wealth, but you may be assured that he or she is rich in the things that cannot be measured with money. When a gift of what is available is offered with generosity, it should be graciously received with gratitude.

If a person were to refuse the gift or meal, it would be considered a slap in the face, bringing shame on the family who offered the hospitality or generosity. The natural sharing of all that one has is an Indian trait that many other cultures cannot or do not understand. Receiving graciously honors the host family. The family's invitation alone shows guests that they are welcome and invited to share.

NIGHT SKY

In the profound darkness,
I touch the face of
    the star-filled Medicine Bowl.
The night sky opens unto me . . .
Creation courses through my woman form.
The pulsating light of stars dance,
        animating the male within.
My senses scream with aliveness.
Exploding stars
    light the fires
        that border this path
            of rapture, still becoming.
The womb of night sky beckons,
    the silent birth of that which
        has not yet taken form.
Diving deeply into the Void,
    without any comfort or guarantees,
        I learn to trust the eternal process.
The beauty of emergence is a mystery
    that I can joyfully endure,
        knowing that it will bring me home.

FORGING THE BALANCE

The fire of youth is impetuous, spontaneous, fearless, and passionate, yet untempered. The passing of winters can bring cynicism, coldness, hardened hearts, and lack of daring.

Fortunately for humankind, there are Elders who cherish the passion of youth, tempering it with the wisdom of age. These Wise Ones refuse to cower in the shadows of lost dreams. On their paths, they refused to bow to hopelessness, refused to adopt the lackluster attitudes of the masses, and stood in the aliveness they saw in the natural world.

Only the bold and the brave seem to be willing to honor the aliveness they carry. They hold the secret of forging the balance of fiery passion and ageless wisdom. They lead through living and sharing their spontaneous perspective, never expecting others to follow. The promise of tomorrow is secure in the hearts of these individuals, because they drink the beauty of all that life has to offer, sharing their aliveness and thanks for that nectar every moment of every day.

SETTING SUN WOMAN

Keeper of tomorrow's dreams,
Mother of the star-filled night,
Show me how to live my truth,
And bring my dreams to light.

Teach me how to use my will,
Living the truth I find within,
Discovering all the parts of me
Where light and shadow blend.

Let me sing the song of future
With concern for what will be,
Upholding all of nature's laws
For creatures, stones, and trees.

Mother, I see you in the sunset,
I hear you in the rain;
You teach me inner knowing
Through your heart's sweet refrain.

Setting Sun Woman, the Clan Mother of the Ninth Moon Cycle, is the Guardian who holds the changing dreams of tomorrow. These changing dreams are constantly in motion and a state of flux because of the shifts in human consciousness. When the human collective changes and grows, the potential for future expands in kind. If we contract and refuse to heal the negativity within us, the future potential implodes. Setting Sun Woman reminds us that separation and fragmentation of the Self can result in dismal consequences for future generations. We do have choices. We cannot change others, but individually we can reclaim our wholeness. Every individual comprises one equal part of the whole. When we heal our lives and cherish the wholeness we have personally attained, we positively affect the future. Is it time to provide for the generations that will follow you by making your healing choices today?

WHAT IS THE WILL?
✄

The will is the emotional body. Intuition, gut feeling, inner knowing, and sense of perception are all directed by our will. When we look at the will to live, we are talking about desire to heal and recover. When we talk about willpower, we are expressing the desire and determination to do something. The first step of creating anything is desire, the next step is decision, and the next step is taking action.

If we have lost our desire, we have lost our will. On any level of human experience, we can discover the places where we cannot seem to make decisions. Because we've been wounded in these areas, we've lost the desire to create or to take action regarding these personal issues, leaving us feeling helpless or hopeless. Human beings can lose parts of their will every time they experience trauma or loss and go numb. When we locate feelings that hold hopelessness in place, we have located an area of lost will. We can reclaim our lost will by feeling everything we blocked at the time of the incident, moving the feelings and letting them go after we feel them fully. The numbness disappears, and we experience a return in energy.

Setting Sun Woman, the Clan Mother of the Ninth Moon Cycle, is the Keeper of Will. She promises us that tomorrow will arrive in fine form, if we do our inner work today. The process of preparing today for the future also includes the idea of what we intend to will, as our legacy, to the generations yet unborn. If we heal the dysfunction today, it will not be passed on as an unwanted endowment. The next Seven Generations deserve a better world, and so do we. Is it time to locate where you have numbed your feelings and lost parts of your will?

WHAT WILL HAPPEN?
✖

WHAT WILL HUMANKIND DO IF WE AWAKEN TO A
NEW, TANGIBLE WORLD WHERE FREEDOM OF CHOICE
IS NO LONGER AN OPTION, HAVING BEEN FORGOTTEN
IN ANCIENT TIMES? IF HUMANITY CONTINUES THIS
SENSELESS SEPARATION OF BODY AND WILL, MIND
AND SPIRIT, MALE AND FEMALE, WE WILL ALL DIE OF
SHEER STUPIDITY!

The one gift given to every human being is freedom of choice. Yes,
we oftentimes override our true desires—our will—by choosing between the lesser of two compromises. Yes, there are places where
freedom of choice is limited to "do such and so or die." But there is
still a choice. When we make mental prisons by denying our ability to choose, we have imprisoned the will—choosing instead the
helplessness, hopelessness, stubbornness, and fear that make us
miserable. The Great Mystery reminds us that the alternative to refusing to free our will is deciding *not to be*.

PICTURE OUR TOMORROW

✖

Paint a picture of tomorrow,
With gentleness, in your mind,
Tinting it all with feelings,
Every emotion of humankind.
Be willing to feel every heart,
And the desires it contains,
Including every nuance,
The joy, as well as the pain.
Don't forget to use all colors,
The pastels, tints, and hues,
That represent the wholeness
That Great Mystery can imbue.
Then sculpt the shapes of destiny,
The patterns great and small,
Weaving dark and light in unity,
Yet, unfolding within the All.
But what is the difference
In this world, and yesterday's?
Is it the final ingredient
That changes our former ways?
Reclaimed will and allowing
Makes this tomorrow . . . stand apart.
Unbound freedom of expression,
Illumination . . . the victory of the heart.

SHARING FOOD

When gathering and hunting were the main sources of food for the Ancestors, planning ahead was of the utmost importance. Winters were hard, and many starved if the spring and summer were not used to store what would be needed during the cold moons.

Sharing food has been a tradition among Native People for centuries. The act of sharing food has many lessons. The understanding is that honor and integrity insist that all members of the Tribe are fed, never allowing anyone to go hungry. It does not matter who grew it; gathered it, hunted and cleaned it, food is to be shared. This sharing makes the Tribal Circle strong.

Trusting the Creator to provide for the needs of everyone is one lesson of selfless sharing. Another lesson sharing teaches us is that if the food runs out, we must be willing to share the burden of hunger—equally, instead of some eating and others starving. When we are taught to consider the whole instead of just the Self or immediate family, we have partaken of the feast of spirit that feeds our hearts with the sacredness of sharing.

LIVING THE TRUTH
✂

SELF-DECEPTION HARVESTS THE
DUBIOUS REWARDS OF PERISHING
AT THE HANDS OF EVERY ACT
OF DECEIVING THE SELF.

That far-off feeling of loneliness can come when we have exiled ourselves from living the truth. When we have deceived ourselves for so
long that we no longer recognize the face in the mirror, we have a
long road to walk on our way home.

The illness of wasting away into nothingness, perishing spiritually, comes to those who refuse to be honest with themselves.
Many people allow themselves to tell little white lies, justifying their
reasons. Many people tell big lies to bolster their insecurities. Many
people tell lies because they fear punishment. In every case, the
hands of self-deception are at work, creating fantasies that claim
life force, eventually destroying the individual. The first step in healing this malady is being honest with the Self. Living the truth begins
the moment we decide to tell ourselves, "It's okay for me to quit
lying to me. I won't punish myself for choosing truth. I will honor
myself for my willingness to change."

WHERE DOES TIME LIVE?
✂

The little boy sat at his Grandfather's knees, winding a length of horse hair round and round his thumb. When Grandfather looked up from blending the mixture for his pipe, he observed the little one's sense of frustration. Finally, the young one spoke.

"How many moons does it take for me to grow tall like my cousin Big Bear, Grandfather?"

"Well, almost double the moons that you have lived. Why do you ask, child?"

"I want to be able to ride a pony and hunt. I just can't seem to make time hurry, Grandfather. Maybe I should go visit time and ask for help."

Grandfather fought the chuckle that rumbled in his belly and looked as stern as he could before he replied.

"We cannot find the place where time lives, little one. We cannot hold it back or push it forward. We Two-leggeds are given the task of learning respect for the seasons that pass. We are asked to make every moment and deed of our lives important and sacred. Tomorrow will never come, bringing us joy, if we forget to find the contentment of today."

Pointing to the young one's heart, he said, "Let us find the place where the joy of this day lives, and we will find the happiness that will last for all of your young life's tomorrows."

POSSESSING TIME
⚓

HUMANKIND CAN ONLY POSSESS TIME BY BEING
FULLY AWARE OF THE ACTUAL MOMENT WE ARE
EXPERIENCING. IN THAT MOMENT, WE ALL STAND
IN THE SACRED HUMAN PRESENCE, DEDICATING
OURSELVES TO THE CONTINUATION OF SHARING AND
CREATING THE SACREDNESS OF OUR COMBINED
HUMAN POTENTIAL. WE WELCOME AND BECOME
THE ETERNAL NOW.

Nothingness gives birth to all things, to totality, and to Oneness in the ever-present Now. Without it, we are lost in the illusions of time and space, without direction or desire.

There is a reason that many so-called *primitive* peoples have no concept of time. It allows them to be fully aware of all worlds that exist within the natural world. Timelessness supports their abilities to journey into other realities made of energy, rather than tangible forms. Since they do not need to alter, control, or make time—trying to possess it—they have forever.

Becoming the eternal, through living only in the moment has given the *primitive* human beings of Earth a major advantage: They never worry about past or future; living only in the present, they are authentically free.

DESPERATE CHOICES

Panic-stricken, out of breath,
He cried out in the night.
What can I do, who can I trust,
To understand my plight?

Faced with my weakness,
Confronted with my shame,
There's no sense in excuses,
There's no one else to blame!
I've lost my faith in myself;
I've given away my youth.
Is it too late for me to change?
I need to know the truth!

Desperate choices filled the dark,
Doubt haunted the alley way,
Demons of fear stood ready
To count this soul as their prey.

A bottle went crashing, against the
* brick wall,*
A light dispelled the gloom,
Amidst the smell of alcohol,
One human being—defiantly
* refused his tomb.*

Ancient ancestors stood at his side,
Although he could not see,
Their silent forms pointed the way,
Great Mystery heard his plea.

Gentle arms reached out to him,
Allowing wracking sobs to subside.
Words of comfort opened his heart,
Healing the hopeless image inside.

That night passed, many years ago,
And his will to live remains.
That man stands tall, for all to see,
With his warrior spirit reclaimed.

CHAINS OF EMPTINESS
✂

Poisoned Water was what they called her behind her back. She never failed to cast a scowl at every woman who crossed her path carrying a child. Her empty womb made her jealous of every fertile woman in her Tribe. She rebuked every attempt at friendship and always passed every ugly rumor that she heard about the behavior of other women.

Poisoned Water had an addiction. She inherited her inability to stop her jealous words when she accepted the chains of emptiness. She had become as empty as a locust's shell when she discovered she was barren. She really believed that she was worthless unless she could add children to her Tribe's population. She had become a slave to her own self-hatred, addictively making her self-abusive inner thoughts into harmful words directed toward others.

Just when the other women thought they could tolerate the abuse no longer, something changed. She Who Heals began training Poisoned Water to deliver babies. At first, none of the women wanted her near them, but in time she became loved by every woman of the Tribe. In finding her talents, Poisoned Water was able to break the chains of her addiction to abusive words. Setting Sun Woman had shown Poisoned Water how to use her will to break her harmful habits. Poisoned Water learned to see how her talents could be used to help the children of future generations. From that time forward, the women honored her real name—Clear Lake.

SUBJUGATING ANOTHER'S WILL
✖

USING TONE OF VOICE, PERSONAL INTENT, PHYSICAL
ATTITUDE, EMOTIONAL THREAT, OR INTIMIDATION TO
SUBJUGATE ANOTHER'S WILL IS AN ACT OF COWARDICE.
THE SELF-SERVING COWARD MAY FEEL THAT THE BATTLE
IS WON, BUT, IN TRUTH, NO ONE WINS!

Any time a human being has to resort to trying to win through intimidation, we can be assured that the person is a coward who is using emotional blackmail to exert control over others. Trying to subjugate the will of another person is a tactic used by insecure tyrants. The Divine Trickster has a few lessons for this pathetic individual.

We may be assured that a bigger, meaner bully will come along to give smaller bullies a lesson in their own bad Medicine, but this is not the way of the Trickster. The Trickster insists that the lessons learned are usually from the consequences of one's own actions. By trying to force another's will into submission, the abuser gives authority to their own shadow side, eventually becoming the victim. The Trickster gets the last laugh when the controller becomes the one who is controlled.

If you have been the offender or the offended, take a look at what the punch line in your situation might end up being. Choices are the gift of the will. Don't be intimidated by anyone, don't give your authority away, don't ask anyone else to subjugate their will, and you will always have the last laugh. Then we can learn to play a game where everybody wins!

NOBLE PURPOSE

❌

Never hurt a living thing,
Walk with a gentle stride,
Capturing all the beauty
That mirrors the love inside.

Know that you are a helper,
A traveler along life's road,
Whose noble purpose lightens
The burdens of another's load.

The kindness and assistance
Given as quiet and genuine aid,
With no thought of personal gain,
No debts needing to be repaid.

Directed by a higher motive,
The release of hunger and pain,
Where no Child of Earth is forgotten,
Nature's balance is cleanly sustained.

These are the personal sentiments
Of noble purpose's guiding light.
With today's gifts of time and energy,
Tomorrow dawns, in its glory and might.

Other than large foundations or corporations, the figures on charity donations in the United States tell us that over 85 percent of the individual gifts or donations to worthy causes are given by families whose income is less than twenty-six thousand dollars per year. What can we learn about the lack of noble purpose in those who have been blessed with extensive material abundance? We can send those who have much our prayers so that maybe their hearts will wake up, hearing the call that guides them to find the inner joy of having a noble purpose.

WATER PROPHECY
✖

The oceans, rivers, brooks, lakes, and streams are the blood vessels of the Earth Mother. To poison these vessels, the Givers of Life, is to insure the wrath of Mother Nature.

In these times, the Earth Mother will show her human children her natural ability to correct their crooked ways. Warning after warning will be issued through flood, disease, and loss of life. Until humankind listens and stops poisoning the Mother's blood system, human sorrows will grow.

Many people are committed to using biodegradable soaps and not putting chemicals on their lawns—unless it causes personal inconvenience. If the clothes do not get clean enough or if their neighbors complain about the weeds in their lawn, they stop.

What about the future, after a natural disaster, when their children are sick and crying from dysentery caused from the chemicals that ran from their homes into the polluted waters that they must drink from to survive; will they make the connection too late?

WATCHING THE WORLD

⚔

The stars rotated in the Starry Medicine Bowl of night sky, lighting the vast path of the campfires of the Ancients. The Ancients were the human beings who walked the Earth, then returned to the fiery essence of the stars. Their campfires in the sky mark the path of the Milky Way.

The communal fire crackled as the families sat silently in expectation, waiting to hear the wonders of this night's story. The Grandfather who would do the telling was so old that his face was a web of wrinkles, set with eyes that twinkled like the stars above. He told a story of a sacred dance, one that included every living thing. He told of how every human being had the potential to see brief glimpses of the dance, and how that dance was forever ongoing.

Every dancer heard a different drum song, and every dancer used steps that only he or she would know as his or her own. The movements were varied, but each set of steps had rhythms that animated that part of the Circle of Life. The Grandfather told of how no living thing could see all parts of the dance because all of the parts to the dance expanded and grew beyond the limiting views of every species. Finally, he answered what all the listeners had been questioning in their own minds. What was this marvelous thing?

"The moving, dancing universe is the never-ending expressive form of the Great Mystery. We are of it and in it, unaware of our contributions to the whole. But through the personal will to live, we discover the aliveness we are given, making our individual dances a harmonious part of the whole."

10TH
MOON

CREATE, CREATE, CREATE
✂

The Old Woman taught her grandchildren how to mold the clay into vessels that would teach them about life, serving the children in many ways. The lessons were many, and so she spoke slowly.

"You children may remember that we asked permission from the Earth Mother to remove this clay from the riverbank and give it a new home and a new purpose. Do you know why we did that?"

No answer came from the wide-eyed children at the Old One's side, so she continued.

"This rich yellow clay has a life, children. It is a living thing, and with the clay's permission, it will bend to your hands. The pots or bowls you make will have a life of their own, and each one will have a purpose of serving in beauty. The clay is flexible when it is wet, brittle when it is too dry.

"The Maker of All Life knows that humans are like that clay. When we become self-serving, we grow dry and brittle, because we are removed from the river—the Giver of Life. But when we use our creativity to serve others, our bodies and minds become flexible again. The waters of life return to us through our perspiration and tears. The path of service we follow is rich and fulfilling because we have become round and whole. Then, like these clay pots, the Maker fills us with spirit until we overflow. That extra, overflowing spirit is our creativity—a gift from The Great Mystery. We learn that through sharing our talents and our gifts, they multiply and grow."

SPARK OF INSPIRATION

Spark of inspiration,
Light my spirit's fire,
Let the joy of creation
Be my heart's desire.
Let me flow with the music,
Let me dance my dreams alive,
Let me sing my deepest feelings,
Until the whole world thrives.
Exploding into expression,
My joy takes many forms,
Leaving the tears and sadness
For the warmth of tender arms.
Hold me, sweet Earth Mother,
Soft against your breast,
That I may share the ecstasy
Of my creation's best.

ATTITUDE
✖

My Elders have taught me that anything we do, speak, think, or make is our creation. When we make something with our own hands, whether it is a meal, a drawing, a sculpture, a plan, a written story, a fence, a toy, or a song, the attitude we have at the time we create those things will show forever.

A song may sound happy, but if it is written while the person is too busy, it won't flow for the listener. If a meal is thrown together, the love isn't there and the food will not be as nourishing. If people are angry or resentful when they build a fence, the job may be filled with problems and the fence may hinder friendships with neighbors. Every attitude is invested into our creations. If one fears that the things they have made to sell will not be appreciated, that fear will keep the clients away.

If we change our attitudes and create everything from joy, the happiness allows our creations to touch the lives of others. The missions of our creations are then unhindered, bringing bounty, beauty, and good feelings to all concerned.

SHARE THE WARMTH

The little girl and boy had a Grandmother who was a weaver. The Grandmother spun the wool of her sheep, colored the skeins, and wove wondrous designs into the blankets she made. The Spirits of their land came to life in the Grandmother's blankets and sometimes would come from the blanket designs to dance in the little ones' dreams.

One morning after dreaming of the dancing spirits, the children approached their Grandmother at her loom and waited silently until she came to a place between woof and warp, acknowledging them with her undivided attention. They spoke of their dreams, asking her why the Blanket Spirits had visited, and how the Spirits had come alive.

The Grandmother smiled as she showed the little ones the one thread of a different color that rested at the corner, out to the edge of every blanket she wove. She explained that it was a road for the Spirits to travel so they would never be caught or stranded inside of the designs of the blankets. The Spirits were free to help the blanket accomplish its mission of serving others. The blanket and the Spirits of their land, who danced in the blanket's designs, found wholeness by bringing warmth into the lives of those who nestled beneath. The Spirits brought sweet dreams and taught the dreamers in their care to share the warmth.

DREAMS IN THE WEB
✖

Dreaming of what would serve the Children of Earth, Grandmother Spider saw many things that seemed discordant to the harmony of the whole. She became troubled by the nightmarish visions at the edge of her web. She knew that all of her dreams would comprise the Web of Creation and that all living things would have those experiences that she was spinning into the tangible world.

Grandmother Spider reached out to the Great Mystery and spoke of her concern, asking the Creator to ease her worry.

The voice of the Great Mystery spoke to Grandmother Spider's heart and said, "There is no reason to fear these challenges that have been placed within the Web of Creation. It is through testing and tempering the substance of our human children that they will find their inner strengths and release the weaknesses of their own creative abilities, growing into their potential and their wholeness. The desire to overcome lives within them and fires their ability to create and to grow. Without challenges, the Two-legged humans will never know desire, and without desire, there is no Creation."

CONTINUAL CREATION OF SELF
✖

HUMAN DESIRE IS THE ACTIVE
INGREDIENT THAT CONTINUES TO
CREATE THE SELF, UNLESS THWARTED
BY LACK OF IMAGINATION.

We have all heard of the self-fulfilling prophecy, but few of us realize that our thoughts regarding ourselves are the way that we prophe-
sy our individual futures. Every time we believe that we are too old
to change, too young for our ideas to be accepted, or any other
final judgment, we stand ready to accept our own self-fulfilling
prophecies.

The limiting comments of others, when believed, can destroy
our creative natures. We are potential in action when we are balanced. When we are imbalanced, our natural creativity turns to its
destructive side. When there are human beings who are approaching their hundredth year of life, still creating the Self, by being active
and interested in learning more, it should create *healthy* shame in
anyone else who decides to quit early. Healthy shame is when we
recognize where we made human mistakes and are willing to give
our best efforts, now and in the future, thus becoming accountable
for our former actions.

*Weaves the Web, the Clan Mother of the Tenth Moon Cycle, reminds us
not to tangle our creativity with limiting lies that alter our potential for
living. Have you quit too soon on something you were creating?*

HUMILITY
⚬

The shadow of the hummingbird,
Darting into the flower,
Flickers on the Sacred Earth,
As I wile away the hour.

Here, within the Stillness,
My thoughts return to me.
Is it true that the nectar of life
Is drunk through humility?

The smallest of winged creatures
Is a testament to the truth,
Knowing that its humble love
Outlasts the arrogance of youth.

When we approach Creation with reverence and humility, the joy of creativity is easily accessible. When we think we know it all, our creations fall short, because our arrogance controls the creative flow. How are you approaching the creation of your life?

BOREDOM
✂

The little boy was busy; his face was intently focused on the toy horse he was making from the bones of a former meal. He had received a lock of mane from Spotted Friend, his older brother's favorite pony. He was given a length of sinew from his grandmother, and his mother had contributed a scrap of trade blanket. The face paint was donated by his Grandfather, and his father had given him a leather thong.

In his mind's eye, the tiny warrior could see the bone horse painted with his Medicine symbols. The scrap of trade blanket would make the saddle; the thong would be the bridle. He envisioned the beautiful mane and tail being wrapped with sinew and was happy as he began his creative adventure.

When he was nearly finished, another boy arrived, scuffing at the earth with his moccasin. The little brave cast a glance at the one kicking up the dust and asked him to stop. The other boy complained that he was bored and had nothing better to do.

The creative child looked astonished and finally replied, "How can you be bored? The world is alive. The game the Earth Mother gave us is creating beauty from what we have at hand. Don't you want to show the Creator that you are willing to play?"

SOLVING THE MYSTERY
✖

The intricate designs of the universe form an overall pattern where every living thing has a place and a purpose. Many men and women of science have dedicated their lives to discovering the rhyme and reason of the workings of the universe. The wonders of the natural world offer constant discovery, and these discoveries often change instantly because nothing in the universe is static. All life forms are constantly creating. Because of the constant change in Creation, many scientific discoveries have come to naught.

The Wise Ones of our Native American culture have a saying that applies:

THE GREAT MYSTERY CANNOT BE SOLVED!

SIMPLICITY

✖

The truth is always simple. Creating anything in our lives can be simple if we access the truths that allow us to see the overall picture. The patterns of all life, mirroring the principles of every truth, are found in nature. We can discover these truths through relationship. Everything is dependent on interrelationship; nothing can survive or stand alone. When we relate in a round, spherical, conceptual way to any idea, we can see the overall pattern.

When we look at things in a linear fashion, deducing what the truth is from pieces, we will become confused with complexities because we are not seeing relationship. We are reminded that a circle does not have a beginning or an end. Inside that circle, every known pattern and geometric shape will fit within the whole. In American Indian culture, wholeness is seen through the concept of the Medicine Wheel, representing the Circle of All Life.

The simple truth is that our planet is round, the orbits of the heavenly bodies are circular, and the planets, moon, and sun are spheres. Doesn't it make sense for humans to see all life as traveling on a circular path, emulating infinite wholeness?

WEAVING THE DREAM

Where in the Mystery,
Of silver webs we weave,
Does life become the mirror,
Of dreams we can't deceive?
And where within do we carry
Deep buried fears and pain,
Remembering to let it go,
So we can love again?
Is it somewhere in our essence,
We hold the desire to spin,
Every creative thread that takes us,
Back home, to the heart again?
Awakening weavers of the world,
We're crying for the dream!
The web of life has room for all,
Within its wheel and scheme.
So weave the web of sharing,
Of all we have ever known;
Our dream emerges with caring,
Through the seeds of love we've sown.

CREATING FRIENDSHIP
⋈

When true friendships are created, these creations are real and lasting. Human beings are asked to honor all their creations whether they be pieces of art, dances of celebration, homes, tools, or personal relationships. We create many things in our lives that should be cherished with our caring, our integrity, and our valued esteem.

Friendship is no different from anything else we build. We start by getting to know the blueprint or substance of a person we feel we can trust. Then we share our thoughts and experience with that person, learning the ideas of constancy, caring, and dependability. Each step in a relationship is a creation and a learning experience. Through these shared experiences, we learn whether we can give and receive freely with a trusted friend. We find out whether that person is to be trusted with our confidences, and to what degree we can continue to create the friendship. A person who has earned the rare treasure of a dependable friend has created a relationship that cannot be measured by the value systems of the modern world. To have a friend who does not judge our faults, respects our feelings, keeps our confidences, and is loyal through all storms is a gift beyond worth. That kind of friend is *earned* when we learn to be the mirror reflection of that same goodness, offering to freely share who we are, our hearts, and our dreams with one of like mind.

CREATIVITY AND IMAGINATION
✖

CREATIVITY SOARS LIKE EAGLE, WHEN
BORNE ALOFT ON THE BOUNDLESS
WINDS OF UNBRIDLED IMAGINATION.

Weaves the Web, the Clan Mother of the Tenth Moon Cycle, teaches us that imagination can open countless paths, build entire civilizations, and allow us to create our dreams come true. If we can see or visualize what we want to create, that becomes possible. If we can imagine a thing, it can be implemented. Our creativity is determined by our ability to dream, using our imagination.

If a person, a society, or a culture loses its ability to imagine, it will die a stagnant death—due to lack of creativity. If you believe you are not creative, you are holding on to a lie. Every human being has to create in order to live. We all create when we are problem solving, working, making a meal, using artistic ability, or walking through life. Every form of expression is creativity, and all creative skills can be developed. The secret to excellence is repeating the process as our skill develops.

If you have a problem imagining, just pretend. If you cannot pretend; pretend you can pretend. This will open the doors to dreaming and imagining again, allowing you to rediscover the creativity inside the Self.

IMAGINATION
✄

Imagination takes us
Beyond the worlds we know,
Following the fanciful dreams
That urge us to create and grow.
That which we can imagine
Follows by taking form,
Gently as a summer rain,
Or violent as a thunderstorm.
If we imagine our worst fears,
With creativity—they grow.
If we imagine adventure in life,
Miracles come with the flow.
Great Mystery's imagination lies,
At the core of Creation's flame,
A gift to every human who
Plays life's mystery game.
Where will imagination take us?
Is it beyond all time and space?
Is there courage enough to imagine
An authentic state of grace?
As we break the chains of limitation,
By dropping the patterns we hold,
New horizons beyond our imagining,
Are born, then allowed to unfold.

WEAVES THE WEB

Gossamer threads of life hold me,
Perched between Earth and Sky,
Weaving the web, dreaming the dream,
Through the two worlds I will fly.
With you as my muse, Mother,
I create the substance of dreams,
Allowing the artist within me
To fashion my life with esteem.
I mold the clay of experiences
Into a sacred Medicine Bowl,
Capturing the essence of living,
As it sings deep in my soul.
Your secrets of Creation, Mother,
Have taught me when to destroy
The chains that have bound me,
Limiting the expression of my joy.
You have taught me how to labor,
Giving birth to the visions within,
Setting them free like silver arrows,
Kindling the fire of Creation again.

Weaves the Web, the Clan Mother of the Tenth Moon Cycle, shows us that there is a time and a place for creativity as well as destruction. If we learn how to change gears, using the old to create a foundation for the new, nothing is ever wasted. Is there something in your life that you need to let go of or to destroy in order to break the patterns of limited creativity? If so, there is no time like the Now. Remember, you can use creative ways to drop those old burdens and break those old habits. The ways others have done it may not suit your uniqueness—be inventive!

INFINITE CREATION
✖

THE MOVEMENTS OF THE GREAT
MYSTERY, *BEING* INFINITE CREATION,
ARE EXPRESSED BY LIFE.

Everything in this universe moves, evolves, changes, and grows. To limited, human perception, some of these changes are so gradual, we discount the aliveness contained within. Nothing is static in our world. Everything is animated by the Great Mystery, which is the universe and infinite Creation.

The human need to limit the Great Mystery to physical characteristics, or to address the Creator as being a gender, is a legacy that has stifled humankind's understanding for centuries. Infinite is simply that—without limit. Eternal is simply that—without time. Creation is simply that, desire and manifestation. To separate any part of the whole is to be a party to the human denial of embracing our own creativity. Fear of separation keeps us from using the gift of creative drive without reservation.

CULTIVATING THE HUMAN POTENTIAL
✖

For any culture to survive, the seemingly menial tasks of planting, fertilizing, watering, weeding, and pruning must be done. The Wise Ones see these tasks on many levels of human endeavor.

It is the work of ancient souls to plant the seeds of inspiration, fertilizing budding minds with encouragement. Is it not *the great work* to irrigate growing human spirits with the waters of compassion and forgiveness? To weed out the sense of failure, created by any learning process, is to enrich the potential in humankind's field of dreams. It is an act of generosity to prune the dead branches of limiting ideas, allowing the curious mind, filled with imagination, to bear fruit.

The Earth Mother reminds us that no seemingly menial task is ever what the casual observer perceives.

Does your personal field of dreams need cultivation? Where can you pass what you have learned to others who may need the wisdom of your creativity in order to access their potential?

AMBUSHING CREATIVITY
✄

In the mind of any human being, creativity is a relative thing. Many people say, "Oh, I'm not creative. I can't draw a straight line!" But, if we ambush these same people with the element of surprise, they can become creative beyond belief.

How many times do we see someone who has been confronted with the results of their actions begin to make up forty excuses about why, or why not, something happened? How often do we see a mother, who has a seemingly empty pantry, whip up a meal from leftovers, or what is at hand, in order to feed hungry children? How often do we observe the miracles of gifts appearing when there was no money, parents finding ways to sacrifice in order to make a child's birthday special?

What is the force behind these types of creativity? In every instance, it is different. Behind the creative excuses, we may find fear, justification, or the need to be right. Behind the sacrifice of parents for their offspring, we find love. Behind artistic creativity, we find inspiration. In truth, all acts of creativity are inspired. The inspiration to defend, needing to be right, may come from the ego. The inspiration to create from love comes from the spirit's desire to serve.

What parts of your recent creations were fueled by the ego? What parts of your creations were inspired by your desire to create from joy? What is the balance in these recent creations? Is there something you want to change? If so, you might try creating these changes from the joy found in growth, rather than from judging the imbalances as punishable offenses. Ambushing your creativity does not mean killing it. It means introducing the element of surprise—challenging yourself with new ideas.

WHICH PATH TO FOLLOW?
✖

BEWARE OF ANY PATH THAT
NARROWS THE POSSIBILITIES OF
THE FUTURE THROUGH LIMITING
FREEWILL OR SELF-EXPRESSION.
ANY PATH THAT PERMITS DIVERSITY
OF IDEAS, WITHOUT JUDGMENT,
SERVES HUMANITY AS A MODEL
FOR WHOLENESS.

One test that benefits the decision-making process and allows us to use good common sense is making note of limiting ideas. When any path we choose to follow insists that we must close our minds to new or different ideas, we should run the other way. Control is at work in these situations. The inability of some organizations, groups, or teachers to allow self-expression shows that their motives may not be too healthy.

When we use our common sense, detecting our uncomfortable feelings in situations that ask us to become unidentifiable as individuals, we need to honor these warnings. Creative self-expression, along with the use of common sense, is a good example of our freewill, operating without denial.

THE GALLANT HUMAN
✄

The gallant human expresses
        the fire in the soul,
Using heroic bravery
        in daring to be whole.
High-spirited and dauntless,
        bold—beyond compare,
Inventive and dashing,
        a spirit with a flair.

Having balanced the fears,
    With the lure of the unknown,
The victories are counted,
    As lessons learned and owned.
This is the gallant human,
    Who lives without regret.
A measure for humanity,
    A waking dream we can't forget.

How has your life measured up lately? To reclaim the gallant part of your nature, you might want to make a list of what you regret about the past and then burn it. Your internal fire will then have a chance to return to your spirit, instead of burning up the raw, creative energy you wasted on regret.

FINDING YOUR FIRE
✂

RISK CHOOSING THE UNCERTAIN
INSTEAD OF THE PREDICTABLE, AND
YOU WILL NEVER TIRE OF BEING ALIVE.

Life's deepest command urges us to grow and evolve through probing the unknown, through abandoning the security of the commonplace, and through trusting that if we set one foot on the road of the unexpected, the path will rise up to support our desire to explore.

Expecting anything less of ourselves can convince us to succumb to mediocrity. We can only masquerade behind timid facades, living amateur lives, for so long. Ultimately, the self-created trap will snap shut with a thunderous roar! Those already numbed, tied in the mental straitjackets of absolute and rigid views on life, may not even notice when the trap was sprung.

One solution held by Native Ancestors was to make sure that nobody did the same thing all day, every day. Camp was moved, the scenery changed, the work details varied. People had to forage for food in areas that provided adventure, allowing all to find their personal fire and to use their creativity.

Today, we can choose to vary our experiences by taking alternate routes to work, trying new things, not being afraid of breaking out of the ingrained habits that produce dissatisfaction.

ULTIMATE STERILITY

The members of the Dreaming Societies called a meeting with the Council of Elders. Both the male and female Dreamers had been assaulted with visions that were strange and frightening to them. It was time to open those dreamscapes and discuss the possible meanings with the Wise Ones.

The Dreamers told of strange boxes that flashed moving pictures of human life. The humans in the boxes acted out violent events and used curious objects that the visionaries had never seen. There were children in the dreams who had no imagination or creativity. The little ones sat in front of the boxes watching the pictures. The children seemed listless and afraid of life.

Murmurs passed around the great circle; curious Elders had no idea what the dreams meant. One Grandfather asked, "Did the humans in the moving pictures feel passion? Could they copulate and make more human beings that were born inside boxes?"

One of the Dreamers answered, "I saw a picture of a man and a woman nuzzling. It was obvious that they wanted to couple, but the picture changed to another scene with a woman who held strange-looking dirty clothing in front of a smaller, white box that had a door on the top. I wondered if the nuzzling humans and their passion were trapped inside the second box?"

These Ancestors had never heard of television. Were their fears that humanity would become ultimately sterile founded in truth? Can we afford to become listless watchers of life instead of creative participants?

PAINTING THE PETROGLYPHS

Our Ancestors left a picture trail of their passages upon the ancient stones. These pictures are very sacred to Native People because they mark hundreds of years of our history. The Stone People carry the libraries of all that has passed on the Earth Mother. When the Ancient Ones added to the records by painting the petroglyphs, they used their artistic creativity to show the locations where the events in our Sacred Legends took place.

Today, in many areas, the creativity of these Ancient Ones is at risk. Some of our Ancestors' paintings are thousands of years old, representing the only physical link that Indian People have to the sites the Ancestors held sacred.

The petroglyphs are a living record of creativity. We are asked to look at what *we* will leave for the next Seven Generations. Will we be remembered for our creativity and for our contributions to humankind or for our destructiveness?

CREATION'S CYCLES
✖

Desire sets the stage for
The decision to create,
Setting the will in motion,
Using our passionate traits
To weave our webs artfully,
To draw upon our dreams,
To make it all tangible,
And lace it with esteem.

When viewing our creations,
We may then choose to change
The perspective or alignment,
Adjusting the depth or range.
When the web of our creation
Breathes our dreams alive,
We can see how our passion
Allows our visions to survive.
Therein lies the secret
Of human creation at its best,
A dream containing passion
Will endure—
    then manifest.

CREATION AND SELF-AWARENESS
⚏

Self-awareness is nothing more than facing the Great Smoking Mirror that reflects all of life, seeing the parts of Self that are mirrored in others. These parts of the Self come in every form and with every contact that we have in the natural world. The creative person recognizes how to capture these images and to use them to recreate the former Self into a new potential.

Whether we observe other people, or nature, or scenarios from life, everything can teach us how to grow. When we see behavior that we cannot tolerate, or a role model we want to be like, we can use these examples to create a new awareness within the Self. We can alter our patterns of behavior to reflect the best of who and what we are, noticing what we do not want to be, as well as what we want others to see in us. The Great Smoking Mirror reminds us that everything that we perceive is for a reason. These human beings who notice everything they come in contact with know that there is a reason for every experience. The Mayans were right when they said, "I am another one of yourself."

LOVING THE SPLIT-APART
✂

My muscles ache from knowing you are beside me,
My bones have been sweetly crushed beneath your
body's weight.
My flesh has been severed by your
omnipotent touch,
My heart almost ceases to pump life through
my limbs when I am embracing you,
And my skin melts and sinks into yours as you
wash away my sense of solitude
Then—
My soul rushes from me to become a part of yours,
and we are each other, and shall be . . . until only Great
Mystery remains.
These things you have taught me,
and I believe . . .

NOSTALGIA
✂

Nostalgia for the old ways and times that gave the appearance of perfect harmony can be tricky situations. We can be tricked into re-creating history to suit our idealized images of how it was, disowning the parts that do not fit into our concepts of the good old days.

Longing for the past and its seeming perfection destroys our ability to create the potential sacredness of today. There has never been a time in Earth's history when human existence was free of challenges. If we could create a life without challenges, we would succumb to mediocrity or the bland sameness that robs humanity of its inspired creative drive.

If you find yourself longing for the past, you may have created a nostalgic trap for yourself. Today is waiting for you to wake up and to use your creative drive to embrace the sacredness of life.

Can you afford to be stuck in the past when the potential for happiness and creativity is in the Now?

CHAOS OR CREATIVITY?

No one could follow the frenetic, humming activity of the bees that filled the meadow of wildflowers. The Elders watched as the children tried to follow the multitudes of flight paths with their eyes.

Later, the children sat in a circle and the Elders asked them if they saw any patterns that seemed as if the bees had an ordered method of gathering honey. The children were stumped. They all saw many different ways that the bees swarmed, moved from flower to flower, and returned to the hive.

One Elder told the children that the method that the bees used was internal harmonious creation. The overview looked like chaos, but each member of the hive was allowed to use its creativity and individual way of gathering, without interruption or restriction. The seeming chaos was actually *harmony in motion* because the Bee Tribe worked to support the whole. Each bee created its contribution in its own way, but the result was harmony. This was the bee's lesson to the Human Tribe, that chaos gives birth to harmony when every member is directed by individual creativity and a personal desire to serve the whole.

11TH MOON

WALK IN TRUTH
✂

HOW DO YOU DESTROY A RIGHTEOUS
PERSON? GIVE HIM OR HER *ONE*
FOLLOWER!

This ancient Cherokee saying is truth in its purest form. The Clan Mother of the Eleventh Moon Cycle, Walks Tall Woman, teaches us that we must lead through example rather than asking others to follow us.

The ways of the Indian Ancestors are perfectly clear, applying the truth to today, just as they did many hundreds of moons ago. Sacred Law is not made by human beings. To follow the rules that are made by humans can lead to a crooked trail. Long ago, no Indian would ever question another person's connection to the Creator or that person's visions or dreams. All human beings were, and are, responsible for their connections to Spirit. When we ask for, and are given, guidance and direction by the Great Mystery, it is our responsibility to follow the truth being presented to our hearts. We know that truth by the serenity it brings and the gratitude we feel.

MOUNTAIN LION SPIRIT
✄

Today, I felt myself falling
  in the whirlpools of your eyes.
There was no one there to help me—
    no present time,
      only eternities of space.
But you have never laughed at me
    for getting lost or afraid.
You just let me be,
    and smiled,
      and my spirit grew until . . .
I believed I could touch your face,
      and I wouldn't be afraid
        to be me,
          ever again.

This experience is ultimately personal for each human being, we cannot explain how it affects our lives. If the loss of fear and the ability to stand tall have happened to you, you know it from the core of your being. If it has not happened to you yet, the joy awaiting you will change how you live forever.

TRUE COURAGE
✳

And the young warrior asked, "Grandfather, what is true courage?" After much thought and silence, the Wise One answered, "Well, my son, true courage takes many forms. It is the willingness to listen, it is the strength of conviction, it is the boldness of decision. It can be the will to allow your heart's vision to lead you on your path. Courage can be the will not to falter when presented with distractions or easy, unsure solutions. True courage is the willingness to be honest, to stand tall, to be connected to the Creator, to honor the Earth and all living things with humility. Above all, true courage is *shown* when a person is willing to walk in truth, never hurting another living thing, no matter what the opposition."

WALK GENTLY ON THE EARTH
✄

Once there was a young girl of seven winters who went to her Grandmother, for her heart was very troubled. The little girl sat in silence while her Elder finished beading a moccasin until the Grandmother noticed the child's sadness. When her Grandmother had wiped away the little one's pained expression and furrowed brow by suggesting they walk to the creek together, the child finally spoke.

"Grandmother, I worry that I am not walking gently upon the Earth Mother. I stopped eating so that I would not ruffle her soft mosses or disturb her fallen leaves, but the weight of my body still leaves imprints in her Sacred Soil, and it pains my heart."

The Grandmother was so concerned she stopped walking, knelt down, and took the child into her arms, turning the little girl so that they would see eye to eye. Then, the Old One spoke. "The Earth Mother wants you to grow strong, passing the winters until you will be an Elder, so you must not stop giving your body the food it needs, my child. I have been remiss in not telling you all that it means to walk gently on the Earth. Will you forgive your Grandmother for forgetting the innocence of your youth?" The little girl nodded, and the Grandmother continued.

"To walk gently on the Earth Mother means to walk with respect in your manner, with a twinkle in your eyes, with love in your heart, and praise on your lips, little one. I have been reminded of these lessons through observing you. Yes, my child, these old bones sing because you have been my teacher."

SACRED MYSTERY
⚏

If you took my heart out,
and burned it for an age,

It would be blackened and burned;
and yet,

You could never burn out the trust
and love planted there,

By the hand of the Sacred One
I have come to know.

Walks Tall Woman, the Clan Mother of the Eleventh Moon Cycle, leads through example because she trusts the Sacred Path that the Great Mystery gave her. We are asked to find that same kind of sacred trust and to allow that Divine leadership to light our way in life, even when the direction it takes us is a mystery to our human understanding.

RETREAT AND LONGEVITY
✂

The Wise Woman taught the young women of the Tribe about the purpose of taking a retreat during their Moontimes. She explained how that woman-time was used to reconnect to the Earth Mother and receive the nurturing needed. Her wrinkled face bore the weight of eighty winters, but the gleam in her eyes was a sign that she would pass many more. The Grandmother answered more questions, and then gave the younger women her view of life.

"As I sit in the winter of my Earthwalk, I look back to the times when I took care of my family, nurtured my youngsters, always being one step ahead of their needs. I was so grateful when I could go to the Moon Lodge and get some rest. Over many seasons, I learned how precious that time had become. I took the strength offered by the Earth Mother, taking the stamina I needed to carry on.

"Our retreat times and reconnection to our Mother may be one of the greatest secrets of longevity. When we are filled with Earth Mother's love for us, as her daughters, we can make many sacrifices for others. But we do not sacrifice ourselves or our health, because we take the time to be filled with Earth Mother's love. That love is the one thing that allows us to endure. With that love, we walk tirelessly. Without the Earth Mother's nurturing love and the love of our families, we are weakened and used up—long before the Great Mystery decides that it is time to call us home."

HYPOCRISY

><

WALK YOUR TALK,
DON'T TALK YOUR WALK!!

Human beings have learned that spoken words are cheap, that promises are often broken, and that, in most cases, a commitment is not honored. All races have adopted some ideas about honesty over the years that stem from being taught that lying is easier than telling the truth. We have all heard that actions speak louder than words. Most of us have experienced the disappointment and hurt connected with dishonest behavior or broken trusts.

In the Native American culture, we have a saying: "Walk Your Talk." If people mouth one thing and do another, they are *talking their walk.* In other cultures, that behavior is called *hypocrisy.*

DECISIONS
✂

Long ago, among Indian Nations, when making choices concerned a person's personal path, those decisions were made by the individual. Decisions were made by a Women's Council if they affected the lives of the Life Givers, and by the Braves' Council if they affected the men. Decisions that pertained to the entire Tribe were decided by the Elders along with the Council of Chiefs.

These decisions were made after hearing all the viewpoints and sides of the situation. This process could take many days, but every decision that was made contained the wisdom that would serve all the People. If the decision concerned the whole Tribe, everyone was required to abide by it.

Native People have some reasonable and just rules of thumb that help every decision-making process: Allow all people to grow at their own rate, changing, without force, when they are ready. Then the decisions that they make will be from their personal desire to change the situation they are in.

American Indian people cannot be hurried into a decision, especially if they know that the decision will affect the future generations or another's well-being. Abiding by one's decisions shows devotion, commitment, and how a person walks in balance. If all human beings were willing to be personally responsible for the far-reaching effects of every decision they made, the *snap* decision would vanish.

GOOD ANGER

Anger has a purpose when
It forces us to change,
Making us so tired of
The shallowness of games.
Anger can be creative when,
Through our fury, we see
The blame we placed on others
With whom we could not agree.
Anger can direct our focus,
Allowing true intent to find
The purpose and definition of
The actions that kept us blind.
Anger can bring awakening
To the souls who were led astray,
Replacing their reason for being,
Sending their apathy away.
Anger teaches many lessons,
With viewpoints, never the same.
We can learn to change our attitudes,
Or continue to shame and blame.

If you finally got so angry that you broke a bad habit, instead of a flower vase, you have already discovered the benefits of good anger. If you are still kicking your car's tires or the dog, you probably need a reality adjustment!

EARNING YOUR FEATHERS

Long ago, among Indian Nations, our Wise Ones taught us that we had to *earn* our Eagle Feathers. This meant that we were judged by our actions, which showed whether we were worthy of wearing the Medicine contained in Eagle's feathers. Acts of kindness, unselfish generosity, caring for those in need, and being good role models for children emulated those high ideals. Eagle feathers were not passed out indiscriminately to anybody who wanted to dress up their regalia.

Today, we are asked to observe how people are walking their lives, and how we are walking ours. Are the people who use their lives to help others being honored? Are we too busy to see the value of those who are earning their Eagle feathers? Have we forgotten to acknowledge them for the role models they give humankind? If others have walked tall, influencing your life, it may be time to let them know how deeply you are grateful. If they had not walked tall, would you know the difference between earning respect and expecting the world to contribute to you?

HONORING THE RIGHT *TO BE*
✄

When we stand in truth,
*   we stand in the light*
*   of Grandfather Sun.*

The roots of our truth grow deep
*   in our Earth Mother's breast.*

Our backs are straight,
*   like the trunk of the strong oak.*

Our hearts are pure,
*   and we fear no human being.*

Every living thing has a Sacred Point of View. When we respect those viewpoints without having to inflict ours upon another, in order to change them, we have learned respect for the Sacred Spaces of all life forms. When we fear another's ideas or way of being, we have lost the connection to our own truth. When we can hear the voice of truth in our hearts, there is no room for fear. We can follow the truth we carry, knowing that we are walking in balance. This kind of truth hurts no living thing, finds joy in the commonplace, celebrates life, and honors all the pathways that lead to inner peace and world peace. Whose right to be have you been honoring lately?

JOY RECLAIMED IN RETREAT

Having lost life's sparkle,
I walked
To the Moon Lodge—alone,
There to find some serenity
I could call up when the need arose.
I witnessed the miracle of reclamation,
As I counted my blessings once more,
My joy returned,
Overflowing,
As through the silence,
I bore witness
To the miracles
I had forgotten in my haste:
Tonight the moon burst!
Yesterday, I taught a child to smile.
This morning,
I found a rainbow on my doorstep.
Tomorrow,
I want to share my joy with you.

*Walks Tall Woman, the Clan Mother of the Eleventh Moon
Cycle, reminds us that there is strength in retreat. Sometimes
that strength can mean the difference in how we view our lives
and the joy we are offered, if we make the time to receive.*

WORKING TOGETHER
✖

In order for everyone to be fed and clothed, every member of a Tribe had to do what he or she could to contribute to the whole. Working together was one of the ways in which a person's character could be observed firsthand. If the willingness to contribute was a part of the person's makeup, it was easy to identify.

If people had to be asked to help others, it was a sure sign that they had not developed the gifts of working in unity. Depending upon others to do the work, while reaping the rewards of others' labors, was looked upon as a bad character trait. Those who worked with a happy heart and gave of themselves without complaint were considered valued members of the Tribe.

Walks Tall Woman, the Clan Mother of the Eleventh Moon Cycle, teaches us the value of working with others in unity and with joy, leading through example by being a contributor.

THE STRENGTH OF YIELDING
✄

A mighty blue spruce reached over a hundred feet to pierce the azure canopy of sky. My eyes traveled from the top to the base of my tree companion, filling me with wonder as I realized that its body sprang from solid rock. "What strength," I marveled to myself. The stone that supported the spruce was mammoth, yet it was cleaved in two.

I felt something pull the edge of my awareness and I fell into the Stillness, listening. The mighty spruce spoke to my heart saying, "Strength is found in those who yield. The willow bends to the wind and does not break. This Stone Person has yielded to my roots, making way for new life, allowing its minerals to feed my body. Through infinite seasons, the stone will erode, becoming soil. In time, my wooden body, long past its present use, will give succor to those who come after me. We are willing to yield to the process that gives life to the next generations. This is our strength. We serve during all the stages of our lives. That is the strength found in yielding—we let go of how it is *supposed* to happen. Tell me, human friend, can you do the same?"

WALKS TALL WOMAN
✖

You walk in beauty, Mother,
Allowing all to see
The glory of Great Mystery
That sets your spirit free.

Guided by the bliss inside you,
Walking it through your deeds,
Never needing another's approval,
Your heart's truth takes the lead.

With focus and directness,
You teach me how to walk,
Balancing thought and action,
Instead of misusing talk.

I stand straight in your presence,
I hold my head up high,
With my feet rooted in Mother Earth,
My arms embracing Father Sky.

Walks Tall Woman, the Clan Mother of the Eleventh Moon Cycle, encourages all human beings to celebrate their human potential, never slouching or sneaking through life to keep from being noticed. She teaches us to celebrate the earthly vessels that house our undaunted spirits—our bodies. We celebrate our physicality through finding our rhythm, grace, and movement. Walks Tall Woman embodies the spirit of excellence— teaching us through example that hard work to develop our natural potential must be combined with healthful rest, laughter, and play. Do you need to be reminded of her lessons today?

CLAIMING THE SELF
✂

Throughout history, humankind has run far and fast from *selfhood*. It has been easier to allow others to think for us, to make our decisions, to determine what suits us, and to tell us how we should live. Humans have been pliably manipulated in order to accomplish the goals of greedy, other-determined rulers, as well as, by "polite" society.

It takes courage and insight to rebel against the mundane existence of not being our own persons. Pack or herd mentality is for the weak willed or the fainthearted. Claiming the Self, and one's own authority to make the decisions that will enrich one's growth, is called the Awakening.

If you belong to that rare, brave group of individuals who are their own persons, you have already reclaimed enough of your freewill to claim your rights as a spiritual warrior.

Those rights are simple: You have the right to *own yourself* by making the most of every opportunity the Great Mystery sends your way!

ADVENTURE AS AN ALTERNATIVE
✖

ADVENTURE IS NOTHING MORE THAN
CHOOSING TO TAKE ADVANTAGE
OF THE OPPORTUNITIES THAT ARE ALWAYS
BEING PRESENTED DURING OUR PASSAGE
THROUGH HUMAN LIFE.

Hearken to dissatisfaction!
Let boredom have its way!
Sacrifice your aliveness,
And keep adventure—at bay.
Become rigid and stubborn,
Until you haven't got a clue,
Of purpose or direction,
About what you want to do!
Give up your desires!
Let go of all your dreams!
Drop-kick your creativity,
And mask your self-esteem.
Look at your master creation,
The statue without a will,
A mind without ideas,
A life containing no thrills.

WHAT SHADOW?

Just as physical shadows grow shorter as Grandfather Sun climbs to the noon sky, so do our shadowy natures recede when we embrace the light, as well as the lightness of spirit we carry.

The more clarity and understanding we bring into our consciousness, the fewer telltale shadows of regret, seriousness, and self-abusive behavior we may have following us. It is easy for us to justify our behaviors and say, "What shadow?" That response is usually dictated by our need to ignore any need for growth or improvement. Old habits die hard. Old ways of thinking bear the marks of conditioning. Old fears plague every moment, thwarting our potential for delightful growth.

If we discover our personal desires for change, we have accessed the sunlight needed to examine what no longer works in our behalf. Positive change is the tailgate of the desire to better our lives. That tailgate swings open behind us and knocks the shadow to its knees.

Walks Tall Woman, the Clan Mother of the Eleventh Moon Cycle, shows us the comic relief we can access through our willingness to break the chains of stagnation. Are you daring or irreverent enough to stand tall, knocking regret, seriousness, and self-abusive behavior to their knees? Start by using your lightness of spirit, laughing at any thought that insists that you should punish yourself for being wildly irreverent!

INNER CONFLICT
✖

NOTHING IN OUR UNIVERSE CAN EXIST WITHOUT
ITS OPPOSITE BEING PRESENT. TO JUDGE ANY OPPOSING
FORCE, CONTRARY, OR REVERSE, IS TO GIVE WAY TO
INNER CONFLICT. WITHIN THE BOUNDS OF INNER
CONFLICT, THE SELF'S POTENTIAL FOR WHOLENESS IS
SACRIFICED—THE HEART CORE OF SERENITY BEING
CUT FROM THE WHOLE.

Walls Tall Woman, the Clan Mother of the Eleventh Moon Cycle, reminds us that we cannot Walk in Beauty or in balance if we negate the need for other points of view. The opposites in our world are often the complementary forces that give us varied experiences of human life. By removing one single part of Creation, we could unravel the whole, leaving us with very boring, unchallenging lives indeed.

The question remains: *Would we really be willing to live with the consequences by personally removing any part of human experience that could rob all other human beings of the opportunity to experience every part of life? Playing the part of being that kind of omnipotent judge surely holds unimaginable consequences. Would you want to be held accountable for the results of that kind of judgment?*

THE RELENTLESS LONGING FOR LIFE
✂

Nothing impressed the arrogant young warrior. He always had some kind of comeback for the other young braves who shared in the summer games of their Nation. He excelled in stick ball, he rode his pony with the ease of a seasoned warrior, he matched strength for strength, but his know-it-all, superior attitude repulsed others.

Many moons passed with no improvement in his behavior, until one season's buffalo hunt. The irritating youngster had become a man, having hunted with the men for two seasons. The Tribe's experienced hunters worried, because this brave was never considerate of the consequences of being a loner. He finally paid the price of being gored by a bull buffalo, because he was not willing to work with his Brothers, observing the rules of safety.

Nothing helped the infection that wracked his body. The Holy People were baffled. In a high fever, he cried out for help. The spirits of the Ancestors answered him, saying, "You have never appreciated life and the opportunities you were given. You have scorned others because their gifts were hard earned, while yours came easily. You took everything for granted, but now you have the opportunity to change. If you embrace humility and the relentless longing for life that insists that you appreciate every breath you take, you will heal."

From that moon of healing blossomed a man who became gentle *and* strong, compassionate *and* humbly talented. He earned a new name among his people. He was later called Longs for Life.

APPARENT FREEDOM
✂

The long-winded expert
  Labeled and explained
Every single concept
  'Til no questions remained.

The apparent freedom of
  The knowledge he had gained,
Left him alone and friendless,
  His intellect making him vain.
The fountain of information
  That he wielded like a knife
Cut out every possibility
  Of sharing his feelings or his life.

"What a waste of a brilliant mind,"
  They said, behind his back,
"A heartless encyclopedia,
  The perfect egomaniac."

When love finally found him,
  Doddering and alone,
His years of reflecting
  Brought reality home.

He was more than ready
  To be humble and kind,
For his heart had tasted victory
  Over his ego and his mind.

INDECISIVENESS
✂

INDECISIVENESS IS ONE WAY THAT PEOPLE TRY TO
PREVENT OR TO HIDE THEIR MISTAKES UNTIL THERE
IS NO WAY TO CORRECT THEM. THIS INABILITY TO
COMMIT TO TAKING ACTION IS ULTIMATELY AN
ACT OF COWARDICE.

Governments, bureaucracies, and corporations are often fraught with indecisive people. The fear of losing credibility or status keeps the fainthearted from making decisions that could change things for the better. Hence, we deal with indecisiveness that leads to no positive action or to stagnation.

The decisive people of our world have the courage to take action, fall on their faces, admit the mistake, make it right, and then get on with life. These bold individuals don't count such situations as failures; they gain new skills, learning to walk tall.

In Native American culture, a courageous example of decisiveness is found by recalling when our braves going into battle cried out, "*It is a good day to die!*"

PARASITIC BEHAVIOR
✖

The parasite only lives through taking its life force from another organism. Parasitic behavior in human beings is reflected in the *taker* who cannot give back or will not contribute to anyone else's survival or well-being. These types of human beings have no sense of altruistic conscience. Their sad, victimlike stories, and their need to be supported, are only masking the parasite within.

Testing such an individual is easy. If they are willing to be taught how to support themselves, and are willing to contribute without having to be asked, they are not parasites. If they leech energy from others and make up stories about why they cannot get better unless you do it for them, watch out! The good-hearted often get sucked into situations where they are giving away their life force and becoming weak, unable to bear others' set of burdens.

It takes strong people to walk their talk. Walking tall, in this instance, is having the strength to stop being a host for leechlike individuals. Then the next step is in admitting that we sometimes take care of others so we will not have to turn and face the parts of ourselves that could use the same kind of nurturing care.

In ancient times, those who refused to contribute to their Tribe's survival were banished or left to go hungry. Takers had no honor, and neither did those who would help those individuals steal life force from the community without giving in return.

DISCIPLINED BY JOY
✂

The young man rode his pony from the big meadow up to camp, jumping off at his Grandfather's lodge. He scratched on the hide door, leaving his anger at himself outside, in the burden basket, next to the lodge's flap. Grandfather called him inside, and the two began to talk.

The young brave was upset. While riding his pony in the meadow, he could not hit the center of the brush buffalo the boys had made for a target. The agony on his face made him look older than his eleven winters. Grandfather was sensitive to his concerns, understanding how awkward young hands, jostling on a pony, often slipped when handling arrows and a bow. Grandfather spoke with concern.

"Spotted Horn, when you learn any new skill, it requires patience and discipline. The brave who can see what he may one day become, approaches the learning process with joy, knowing that every victory over his growing body's awkwardness brings him closer to being a full-grown warrior. That vision of himself, and his inner knowing, is the hidden joy. No other person knows what he knows about himself. He carries a secret that makes *being a dedicated disciple to his future potential* an act of happy determination."

TRUE LEADERSHIP
✖

Some leaders and politicians use devices that make them appear to be comfortable around all types of people. These leaders use methods to change their appearances and attitudes to fit the situation, placing emphasis on the seeming interest they have in a particular culture or the problems facing the group they are addressing. Non-Native cultures call this ability "*the common touch.*"

The Native American Ancestors tested their leaders, insisting that their leaders saw themselves as a part of the Circle instead of being above the people. These leaders served the people through their generosity of spirit and their ability to listen and make wise decisions. These leaders served through the understanding that no person was common—all were extraordinary. Each individual was important, and all leaders knew that they could not lead through example unless they humbly loved the humanity represented in every human being.

If you have placed yourself above others instead of being an equal part of the Circle of Life, you may want to adjust your perspective. Leading through example is a road that only the authentically humble can actually master.

FLEXIBILITY
✄

Sitting in the lodge, the Chief spoke to the Warrior Clan, expressing his wisdom in a way that touched each brave's heart.

"The warrior who understands flexibility will be able to serve the People to the fullest extent of his abilities. The body must be strong and agile, limber and conditioned, so it can carry out the decisions made by the mind. The mind must be quick and focused, free to make instant decisions that could save a life. The spirit must be flexible enough to grasp the intent of the Great Mystery, as well as the visions and Medicine the Spirits bring our way. The warrior who knows these things and keeps himself flexible will bring honor to the People. The final lesson of any warrior is in understanding the will. Every warrior must be flexible enough to feel and express the emotions that come to him, without being governed or controlled by feelings that would lead him to dishonor his solemn vow to be a protector of the People."

If momentary anger or other upsetting emotions could cause you act rashly, take a breath and be flexible. Feel and release the emotions that cause imbalance. A spiritual warrior seeks balance and solutions in every situation. Your honest intent to be a good role model could be at risk.

REPUTATION

Our actions tell a story
To observers who view
The honesty and intentions
Found in everything we do.
The basis of any reputation
Will sound its own alarms,
Measured by expected behavior,
Through honor, or through harm.
Every life tells its story,
Every human draws the lines,
The boundaries of personal honor
Are ours to live and redefine.
Jealousy, hatred, and poverty
Can prey upon human souls,
Tarnishing the spirit's intent
To reach an honorable goal.
But finding the path to healing,
And seeing self-worth inside,
Can change a bad reputation
To one of honor and pride.
If your past still haunts you,
It's time to give it away,
Live the best of your potential,
By leading through example today.

INITIATIVE
✂

THOSE WHO FEAR INNOVATIONS, CHANGES IN
OLD ROUTINES OR OUTDATED HABIT PATTERNS,
ARE ACTUALLY AFRAID TO TAKE INITIATIVE. BEING
A SELF-STARTER ALLOWS ONE TO HAVE A BLOODLESS
WEAPON THAT DESTROYS THE DEBILITATING
DISEASES OF STAGNATION AND BOREDOM.

Native Ancestors encouraged every person to be a self-starter, telling stories of how the lazy and the uninspired ended up following crooked trails that led nowhere, resenting others who had the courage to achieve their potential. If we look deeply into the causes for lack of initiative, we will find fear stalking those who cannot seem to get on with life. That unrelenting terror can contain fear of failure, fear of ridicule, fear of not having the stamina to complete what was started, or fear of not being worthy. In all cases, the shadow side of human nature wants us to believe that we don't need to try.

If we opt to take the easy way out by never making an attempt to stretch beyond our zones of comfort, we will never know the joy of standing on top of the mountain, viewing all the trails we have climbed to reach the power that is hidden in our potential. Have you given yourself a chance to stretch lately?

BLESSINGS OF LIFE

I have seen the spotted ponies
Run 'cross miles of open plains.
I have heard the Rainmaker
Sing for thunder and rain.
I have danced with Kachinas
Deep within my dreams.
I have walked the Golden Earth,
Reaching for sunbeams.
The Ancestors speak to me,
Their spirits on the wind,
Reminding me to be grateful
For the blessings Creator sends.
With beauty all around me,
My heart is full of praise,
For I have seen the wonders
Of the Earth Mother's ways.
Each sunrise is a blessing,
My shelter, the open sky.
Earth Mother fills my heart,
Until like Eagle—I fly.

Gives Praise, the Clan Mother of the Twelfth Moon Cycle, teaches us to never take anything for granted. When we show gratitude for all the simple joys of life, we make the space for more happiness to enter our lives. When we forget to show our thanks, by taking life and breath for granted, we can lose the precious happiness that has guided our ability to receive further blessings.

COUNTING BLESSINGS BY
RETURNING THANKS
✄

GIVING THANKS FOR EVERY BLESSING OF BEING
ALIVE REMINDS US OF THE PRIVILEGES WE ARE GIVEN
THROUGH THE PLEASURES OF PHYSICAL LIFE.
TO TAKE THOSE PRIVILEGED BLESSINGS FOR GRANTED
IS TO WELCOME THE DISCONTENT OF OTHERS
WHO FEEL THEY NEVER HAVE ENOUGH.

Gives Praise, the Clan Mother of the Twelfth Moon Cycle and the Keeper of Gratitude, shows us the way to abundance by teaching us that the gifts of health, perception, warmth, shelter, air, water, food, trustworthy friends, and a loving family are to be counted as blessings. These precious gifts could be taken away without notice and never counted until removed. True wealth is never counted by any person in exactly the same way, but the wise person realizes that the basic needs of human beings are the authentic blessings that symbolize true wealth. The other trappings are easily let go of, becoming former illusions and delusions, especially when the things we depend upon for survival are at stake.

TO LIVE WELL
✖

THE ANCIENT ONES HAVE TAUGHT US THAT EVERY
LIVING MOMENT IS PRECIOUS, EVERY THOUGHT
CONTAINS CREATIVITY, EVERY DECISION DIRECTS
OUR LIFE FORCE, AND EVERY ACT OF PHYSICAL LIFE
IS SACRED. TO KNOW THESE THINGS, AND TO
WALK THESE TRUTHS, IS TO LIVE WELL.

We are taught by Gives Praise, the Clan Mother of the Twelfth Moon Cycle, to celebrate our lives with dance, ceremony, Rites of Passage, and feasts. These are some of the rewards we can share with those we love, marking the events that have given us reason to rejoice for the blessings in our lives.

When we forget to honor those who accomplish things, we negate the effort it took that person to live well. When we forget to show our approval of a job well done, through praise and encouragement, we have lost our gratitude. Living well insists that we share our good fortune through generosity and caring. Is there something or someone you have forgotten?

ADMIRATION

Admiring a flower allows that blooming plant to feel appreciated. Admiring the beauty in a sunset gives the Earth Mother and Grandfather Sun a sense of the viewer's gratitude. Admiring other humans for the good choices they make, the kindness they show others, and for their accomplishments is the sign of a wise person. For in admiring another, the wise person is honoring another's life, as well as the spirit who directs that life with goodness.

When we admire the natural world, we are returning thanks to the Maker of All Life and each individual part of Creation. When we praise a job well done or when we admire the way that a human being walks through life, we are showing our pride in another, letting the person know that he or she has earned the right to be appreciated.

Have you been encouraging toward those who are living treasures in your life lately?

Have you taken the time to tell someone who has been a role model for you that you appreciate him or her?

Shouldn't you make the time to show your admiration?

CELEBRATING LIFE
✂

Celebrations were one way that Native American Tribes marked the blessings that came into their lives. The blessings of a successful hunt could be counted as no injuries and plenty of fresh meat. The blessings of a marriage held the potential promise of offspring that would add to the members of the Tribe. The blessings of abundant harvests meant enough food to carry the Tribe through the winter. The blessings of a Puberty Ritual would speak of another child coming of age, ready for the responsibilities of adulthood.

These blessings did not just affect a few people; they affected the whole Tribe because the Tribe worked as an extended family. The survival of the whole depended upon the contribution of the individual accomplishments of every member. To lose one person to illness, accident, war, childbirth, or capture brought great sorrow. Indian People have shared the suffering, the mourning, the blessings, and the reasons for celebration throughout time.

Today, when there is reason to celebrate, everyone is invited to share the food, the dancing, the drum music, the laughter, and the goodness of the blessings received. The family hosting the celebration is showing their gratitude to the Great Mystery by sharing their good fortune with others.

Maybe it is time for all human beings to mark the blessings they receive by celebrating the accomplishments of every family member and then honoring those blessings by sharing with others. The joy is contagious and brings happiness into the lives of others who want to celebrate with us.

USING DANCE AS THANKSGIVING

The children gathered around the Medicine Man as he explained the preparations he was making for the Harvest Dance. One child asked him why the people danced and feasted in the Moon of Red Leaves. He sat the children on tree stumps, in a circle, placing himself on the earth in the center before answering. Looking into the eyes of each youngster, at the level of their line of vision, he was letting them know that they were equal and that their questions were important.

He explained that many members of the Tribe had praised the mission of the seeds, thanking the Earth Mother while they planted the seeds, nurtured the plants, sung and danced for rain. The people had continued to return thanks while the plants grew to maturity. Now, in the Moon of Red Leaves, it was the time of gathering the fruits of the Tribe's labor.

The dance would mark the time of expressing gratitude for the Earth Mother's abundance in providing nourishment for the plants. The dancers would be returning thanks for the sunlight provided by Grandfather Sun, and for the rain, freely given by the Thunder Chief and Cloud People. All of the steps that brought the harvest were to be acknowledged in sacredness. The Great Mystery would see the people's appreciation through the joy in their dance steps. Each step, each song, each drumbeat was sending thanks back to the Creator for the blessings the Plant People would bring through the winter, aiding the survival of the Human Tribe.

REMINDER
❌

Anything that has brought a smile to your lips, joy to your heart, or a lightness to your step is a blessing. Anything that has made your life more comfortable, has lightened your burden, or has brought warmth to your home is a blessing. Anything that has supported your body, increased your endurance, or opened your heart is a blessing. Anything that has made you look deeper, has expanded your understanding, or has increased your compassion is a blessing. Anything that has tested your strength, fortified your commitment, or forced you to grow is a blessing. Anything that has reminded you of how precious life is and has taught you to treasure your Relations is a blessing.

The Creator reminds us that blessings are counted in the way that we choose to look at them.

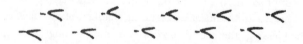

WEDDING GIFTS
✖

Among some Native Americans, it is still a Tradition for the bride and groom to have a Give-away Ceremony for others at their wedding. It may take a long time for the couple to accumulate the gifts and funds for the Give-away and the feast. The guests may have traveled long distances to share in the ceremony. These guests are honored by receiving special gifts for having attended, supporting the couple's decision to wed. The gifts for the guests represent the union of loved ones, giving happy memories throughout the years to those who shared in the Ceremony.

Gives Praise, the Clan Mother of the Twelfth Moon Cycle, shows us how important it is to show gratitude for the people who support our decisions, share our happiness, and honor us with their presence. In the Ways of the Ancestors, it is through giving that we receive the understandings of what our individual blessings hold.

REWARDING ASSISTANCE

In times past, when any family called upon a Medicine Person to perform a healing, a Ceremony, or to give assistance of any kind, that help was rewarded in a generous way.

The family who needed assistance gathered many useful items, such as fresh elk or buffalo meat, beaded moccasins, blankets, baskets, horn spoons, dried fruit and tubers, and many fur pelts. Depending on the area, the gifts would also include tobacco, sage, sweet grass, cedar, or corn pollen. These gifts would be given to the Medicine Person for the work he or she had done for the family.

Today, many non-Native people have asked for assistance from Native American Medicine People and have then rewarded that assistance with a bag of tobacco and less money than it takes to buy a tank of gas. How are these Gifted Ones supposed to feed their families? How will they be able to travel home if it is a long distance? What does this behavior say about the gratitude of those recipients?

Gives Praise, the Clan Mother of the Twelfth Moon Cycle, reminds us that every person in our lives who is asked to help us should be rewarded with generosity. Our actions show the world how much value we place on those who assist us and the amount of gratitude we feel after a crisis has been successfully handled.

RITES OF PASSAGE INTO MANHOOD
✖

The young boy had passed his thirteenth summer when his family called upon a Medicine Man to perform his Rites of Passage Ceremony. The Medicine Man prepared the youngster by conducting a Purification Ceremony in the Stone People Lodge. The steam from the hot stones, sage and cedar smoke, and many prayers cleared the path for the beginning warrior.

High on the mountain, all alone, without a fire for comfort, the young man learned what it was like to rely upon himself. The night sounds filled his senses and brought many fears. The nightmarish pictures created by his active mind made the darkness close in, playing many tricks on him. Finally, he called out to the Creator and was rewarded for his prayer. The little brave felt the comfort of every Ancestor Warrior who had walked the Earth Mother before him. His fear was lifted, and the Great Mystery spoke to his heart.

"Young One, the making of a warrior comes when he is not afraid to call upon the Creator's strength. The road of courage is a path of partnership. Brotherhood depends upon one's willingness to stand in unity with other warriors. The first partnership is made between you and the Creator. You may trust our bond, and you may depend upon that strength. This is the first Rite of Passage that any protector of the People must learn in order to have a fearless heart."

LETTING GO OF LOVED ONES
✂

The passing of a loved one is marked in many different ways by Indian People. In some Traditions, a Burning Ceremony is held where all possessions of the deceased are placed in a pit and burned while the family and friends pray, sing, and dance all night until dawn. This Ceremony is performed to cut all ties between the one passing over and the physical world. The singing, prayers, and dancing give the loved one's spirit enough energy to leave physical life and material possessions, traveling into the Spirit World.

This Ceremony also gives those who stay behind the opportunity to say their final good-byes, letting go of their needs to keep the loved one with them. The act of letting go is as important for the friends and family as it is to the spirit who needs to go on to the next set of lessons contained in the Spirit World.

We are reminded that our desires can be selfish, that our refusal to let go of the ones we love may place our needs before their needs. Our fears and sense of loss may be harboring regrets. That is why we are asked to count each moment with another living person as being sacred. That is the reason we are asked to treat others with respect and love. When we treat others in a shameful way, using words we cannot take back, we may be faced with some very hard lessons when they unexpectedly pass over.

NO FORBIDDEN SECRETS

Long ago, among Indian People, the secrets of the Great Mystery were available to any person who went through the steps necessary to receive a vision by walking a spiritual path. The Ancestor Spirits talked to all who had opened their hearts to receive wisdom. The wisdom was given to those who *earned* the right to know.

Today, the particular steps of healing arts, dances, and Ceremonies specific to individual Tribes and Clans are not public information because they are Sacred Paths to wisdom that have to be *earned* by the members of those Tribes. In many cases, these Native Americans have been prepared since childhood to understand the ways of their People. No member of any Tribe would ever ask to be included in, or go uninvited to, a Ceremony that was not from their Tradition. Those Ceremonies are private and sacred, belonging to the people whose Ancestors created them.

My Elders taught that the Great Mystery gives spiritual wisdom to any human being, of any race, who seeks Tiyoweh, the Stillness. There are no forbidden secrets when a person accesses their personal spiritual understandings by going directly to the Great Mystery. It is up to all individuals to find their own connections to the Creator by following the messages received in their hearts. This allows any seeker to respect—without intruding on—the Spiritual Traditions of others.

FAITHFULNESS

*Faithfulness never turns its back
On a brother or sister in pain,
Refuses to listen to rumors
That envy and jealousy contain.
Faithfulness speaks of abundance,
Listens to problems and woes,
Then offers the healing solutions
Of the Sacred White Buffalo.
Faithfulness knows that devotion
Cannot waver, or be replaced,
For our constancy is reflected
In every deed that we embrace.
Faithfulness weathers the trials
That plague each human storm,
And is willing to go the distance,
Keeping loved ones safe from harm.
Faithfulness is the guardian of
Our trust, our honor, and bond,
Allowing others to depend on us,
Knowing through faith . . .*

    we will respond.

NAMING THROUGH ACTIONS

⚹

Long ago, Indian People were given many names during their lives. These names reflected their growth as human beings. The names given at birth were changed when children passed a certain age, which varied from Tribe to Tribe. Some secret names were given at birth and were never known by anyone other than the child's mother, the Wise One giving the name, and the Creator.

Later in life, a name change would generally reflect some deed that showed a person's temperament, gifts, or basic nature. Not all of these names were met with appreciation on the part of the recipient. A person could be called a new name due to bad behavior as well as good. For the people who received shameful names through their actions, it was necessary to correct their behaviors before another name could be acquired.

Think of the impact on our modern world if all people were named by their family and peers for their deeds. What would the effect be if people had names like Steals Money or She Who Lies, Refuses to Listen or Beats His Wife? What would happen if every human being were stuck with a name that was widely known, until he or she changed the behavior? To find out how your chronic attitudes could name you, take a look at how others see your behavior day by day, finding the truth of what needs healing. What would your family and peers name you today?

GIVES PRAISE
✄

Thank you, Mother, for teaching me
To lift my heart in praise,
Filling my spirit with gladness
For the blessings of the Beauty Way.

You have taught me how to sing,
How to rejoice, dance, and drum,
And how to sing my gratitude
For the abundance that will come.

You have shown me the magic of
A change in the mind and heart,
An attitude made of wisdom
That celebration of life imparts.

I sing the truth of thankfulness
When I greet Grandfather Sun,
Then send my love to Mother Earth
For the life force that makes us one.

Gives Praise, the Clan Mother of the Twelfth Moon Cycle, reminds us that every sorrow contains a blessing, every act of life mirrors a lesson, and every cloud masks an opportunity. If we live our lives in celebration of each tiny blessing, our gratitude will create the space for further abundance. Have you forgotten your priorities by letting yourself take someone or something in your life for granted? Be grateful today. Show that person how much you appreciate his or her presence. Look at how you might feel if the little things were taken away. It may be time to return thanks to the Creator, allowing the mystery of life abundant to find a grateful heart to flow into.

LEGAL TENDER OF THE SPIRIT
✖

What payment does the Great Mystery expect from the spirit? Many world religions have tried to enforce and exact payments in the form of rigid codes, laws, commandments, penance, money, or guilt. These are human-made rules that enforce the payment of what is considered legal tender by various self-appointed religious judges.

In the Indian way, sacrifice originally meant "to make sacred." For the human *spirit* to make every act of life sacred, there has to be gratitude for the opportunities of experiencing life in a physical body. To deny the senses of the body, the pleasure of movement, or the varied experiences of human, physical life is to disavow the sacredness of life on Mother Earth. *If* our spirits sacrificed our freedom by coming into physical form, we all *chose* to make physical life as sacred as life in the Spirit World.

In Native American Tradition, we see this sacrifice as making the realms of Spirit and Earth equal. We understand that the blessings being offered through our physical lives are not a punishment; they are the lessons that allow the spirit to understand the value of Oneness without judgment.

Perhaps we are being asked to give praise, to return thanks, for the opportunities being presented. This is only the payment the Great Mystery asks of us, and even that legal tender is a reciprocal gift that should be gladly returned through the joy of each individual's freewill.

RESERVOIR OF MEMORIES

When any human being drops into the feelings of helplessness and hopelessness, there seems to be no strength left to draw upon. The acute emotional pain associated with loss is a difficult thing to bear. In situations where devastating events have dealt a crushing blow to the spirit, it is often nearly impossible to look at the blessings. We have all heard that behind every difficulty is an opportunity, and at times that may seem to be the case. However, it is very difficult for people who are starving or dying from exposure to believe that there is a bright side to their situations.

The human potential to hang on and to survive is the property of the spirit and the will. A very fine thread of faith is the tightrope that many have to walk daily. This thread can be strengthened through the reservoir of memories. To recall a kindness, an act of generosity, or a happy moment is to access the memories that give us strength in hard times. This ability is a blessing in itself, which, when used regularly, can reinforce determination and the spirit's resolve to make it through. This reservoir is like a bank where we have deposited memories that can help or thwart our intentions to grow beyond hopelessness. Which memories we choose to withdraw from that account is a matter of freewill.

We are reminded that we can feed our strength, or dilute it, with our thoughts. One of the blessings we may count, if we feel hopeless, is the blessing of choice. No one can steal how we choose to think, or our ability to nurture our faith, through calling on the memories of former blessings.

MAKING IDOLS AND GODS

When we look at our modern world, we see that we have made gods of political and spiritual leaders, fame, prestige, and wealth. We have created idols of intellectual ability, physical beauty, and a host of other seemingly desirable things.

The awakened individuals, who have earned the right to speak from the humility learned from their human experience, remind us:

> WE DON'T NEED ANY MORE GODS! WE NEED A SPACE
> FOR SOME MORE HUMANITY IN OUR WORLD!

MARRIAGE OF WORLDS

The wave of a cloud exploded
on the blue shores of infinite space.

I watched as the tide pools,
made of cornflower blue sky,
yielded up ghostly shapes,
matching those creatures who
lived deep in the sapphire seas.

There for all eyes to see
was a marriage of worlds,
reflecting the oneness
of watery births, of sky—mirroring sea.

My body formed the connecting link,
an antenna for Creation's great beauty.

My task was to celebrate
that beauty's transmission,
sharing my unexplainable feelings of union,
trusting in my heart of hearts . . .
that others, would choose to feel it, too.

PASSAGE THROUGH IMBALANCE

The Great Mystery gave the Red Race a gift of wisdom, so that we could understand the ideas of unconditional love. Originally, in Native American Tradition, there was no word or idea for "sin." The concept of imbalance is as close as the Ancestors ever came to the idea of sin. There is no judgment in the idea of imbalance, because imbalance implies a need for healing, and can be corrected.

Instead of judging another for sins or spiritual crimes, we look at what needs to be healed to bring the individual back into balance. People who are out of balance are allowed to discover the crooked trail they are following when they fall down, become ill, or their inappropriate behavior is reacted to by others. It takes great courage not to meddle in the affairs of others, but rather to show them the value of unconditional love, revealing healing examples of balance through one's own actions. It becomes a Rite of Passage for the imbalanced, as well as those who love them, showing all concerned the lessons of loving unconditionally.

GRATITUDE FOR COMMUNITY

The gratitude for Tribal community has always been apparent in Native American cultures. The gift of a functioning, supportive social community that survived by using loving cooperation was our Ancestors' way of life. Those ancient Tribal communities used mutual aid and the understanding of group survival to bond all members together as family. The lack of separation and selfishness allowed the Ancestors to survive many a hardship.

Today, the focus of every human being who wants the end of separation should be on these same kinds of mutually supportive concepts. If humankind could achieve these same goals, even in small communities, we would be able to make an enormous impact on the overall planetary picture.

Many seers, visionaries, and Dreamers have seen the potential for the Human Tribe to come together in harmony. We are now facing the ultimate Rite of Passage in that process. No matter how bad it looks in our world, we must show our gratitude for the daily changes in the hearts of human beings that are realizing that they are vessels that contain the Great Mystery's love. When that part of the Rite of Passage is clear, it then becomes evident that all human beings are family: one Tribe—all very human, all in need of some kind of healing, and all in need of understanding the potential for community, *communication in unity.*

Support this potential for the reunification of the Human Tribe by returning thanks for every human being who embarks on this Rite of Passage; then, be willing to live your commitment to unity.

THE TAME HUMAN
✖

The cavemen had a knack
For survival and the hunt,
But behaving like animals,
Their women bore the brunt.

Cro-Magnons changed the memory,
Carried in the blood, not the brain,
Replacing the hairy Neanderthals,
Our bodies reflect all that remains.

Now we face the tamed human,
Who through luxury has become
A proclivity of the intellect,
With the instinct growing numb.

What happened to drive and passion?
Did couch potatoes forget to feel?
Have the tamed humans given away
The wildness, to become genteel?

Gives Praise, the Clan Mother of the Twelfth Moon Cycle, reminds us that
complacency keeps us from capturing the best of life that comes through
aliveness and feeling. If we can't laugh at the tame, emotional fences we
build to protect us from exploring life, we are in trouble. Every Rite of
Passage in human evolution has brought us the victories and the setbacks.
Have you been taming a part of yourself in order to fit in?

ENCOURAGE THE POTENTIAL
✄

The yellow moon hung low in the horizon, mirroring the golden glow of the desert haze. The old woman gathered the last of her twigs and adjusted the burden basket on her shoulders, preparing for the walk back to her lodge.

Suddenly, her senses were alert. A mewing sound was coming from behind a dune. There was a human, crying but trying to muffle the sounds. The old woman cautiously peered over the dune, discovering Wants to Walk, a young woman of her Clan. After much cajoling, the old one found out that Wants to Walk had been made fun of when she tried to weave a basket, her young hands not able to instantly master the art. The old woman comforted the girl child and finally took her home.

The following morning, the old one called the women together and had her say. Her words were razor sharp.

"The young people have a deep, natural desire to learn, especially when they are encouraged. When anyone belittles their efforts, their desire can be killed and buried forever! Wants to Walk showed that desire when she was a baby and could only crawl, but she tried to stand and walk no matter how many times she fell. It is time that we all remembered to encourage the potential we see in everyone. To scorn honest effort is an act of cowardice. Through scorn, we show our fear that others have more talent than we do!"

PETTY TYRANTS

THE LITTLE-MINDED PEOPLE WHO SEEK POWER
OVER OTHERS NEVER USE ENCOURAGEMENT. THESE
DEVIOUS, PETTY TYRANTS WORK DILIGENTLY TO
DESTROY THE FAITH THAT OTHERS HAVE IN THEM-
SELVES, USING CRITICISM AND COVERT HOSTILITY
AS THEIR EQUALIZERS.

Pettiness is a tragic shadow part of human nature. When people are so insecure that they have to belittle another, the shadows of self-rejection and self-hatred have a field day. It is evident to the astute observer that the same covert actions used on others are undermining the petty tyrant as well.

The shadow keeps the jealousy circulating inside the little-minded in order to manipulate and control their despotic behavior. It works! The ones who want control over others never realize that they are being controlled by their own shadowy natures. In seeking to destroy others' faith in themselves, the power-hungry or insecure human has unknowingly undermined the Self's potential for true greatness.

PRAISING THE FLOW

THE WISE PERSON PRAISES THE UNIVERSAL FLOW OF CREATION. INSTEAD OF FINDING FAULT WITH WHY THINGS ARE NOT GOING THE WAY ONE CHOOSES, THE TRUTH SEEKER WILL REFINE THE ABILITIES NEEDED TO FIND THE NATURAL FLOW, AND THEN GO WITH IT.

If we are not in sync with the natural flow of life, we may be controlling or manipulating events, or our behaviors, to reach a desired outcome. The stronger the control, the less chance we have of experiencing the effortlessness of synchronicity. Complaining adds to the problem, because we waste the energy that could be used to refine our abilities, wasting our access to the natural flow.

When we return thanks for the pulsating rhythms of Creation, we acknowledge the natural flow. That flow is then easier to relate to and to be a part of. The blessings we receive when we allow the natural flow to guide us are all of the gifts of effortless, creative living. The river of life is always inviting and encouraging us to get into sync, and to *go with the flow.*

The questions still remain:

> Can we authentically allow ourselves to trust the flow of Creation?
>
> Or is it easier to waste life force on trying to control the outcome?

SACRED WORDS

These were desperate times for the families of the hunting party that was lost in the blizzard. The Elders called on every member of the Tribe to pray for the safe delivery of those stranded in the snow.

Sacred words cut through the storm, sending strength to the hunters. The warmth of Great Mystery's breath kept the men from freezing. Many of the stranded men had visions of Ancestor Spirits building fires around them, with invisible buffalo robes being placed over them to protect them from the bitter cold.

When the hunting party returned home, revealing the mystical experiences they had encountered in their hour of need, the Medicine Elders smiled. They knew the power of the sacred words, and the intent those words carried, had reached beyond the physical restraints of reality.

An Elder nodded and said, "There is no limit to the partnership between humankind and the Great Mystery. Our faith and our intent, coupled with the Creator's boundless grace, make any situation that seems impossible a challenge we can overcome."

ALLOWING AND NONINTERFERENCE
✄

The intent of one who prays for another is oftentimes fraught with personal desires for another's well-being. When we pray for a desired outcome in another's life, we can be interfering with freewill, as well as that person's place in the Divine Plan.

When we ask for healing for another, it is best to be neutral as to how that healing is to take place. When we pray that another person can find the strength to change, we need to allow that person freewill concerning how, or if, they choose to make these changes. If we return thanks for the love and guidance that is being offered to another person, and ask that the gift be recognized and used for the highest good, we have practiced noninterference. When we send loving thoughts to another, without judgment or criticism, we have allowed that person freedom of choice. Without expectations or demands, there is no need for people to rebel, hurting themselves or another in the process, demonstrating the need to be rid of unwanted, outside interference. Well-meaning intent often takes the form of controlling behavior, when we could just as easily turn those worries over to the Creator. Divine Intervention happens when we get out of the way and allow.

Is there some area of your life that you can let go of long enough to allow Divine Intervention to happen?

INNERMOST SENSE OF PURPOSE

The sacred flow within us
That draws us into life
Teaches us to be grateful,
For the blessings and the strife.
The path of human experience
Is based on our desire to be,
Using the bitter, and the sweet,
To form a balanced reality.
The innermost sense of purpose
Is in grasping the eternal flow,
Stepping on the path with praise,
Respecting how we learn to grow.
Feeling the pull of Creation,
As it beckons, calling our names,
Setting aside all separation,
Praising the Oneness we reclaim.
Is our secret, innermost purpose
To mend the polarity within?
Can we find human wholeness
And allow separation to end?
Each individual holds the answer,
And each spirit must decide,
To praise the truth of Oneness,
Allowing ultimate unity to abide.

13TH
MOON

MOON OF TRANSFORMATION

Oh, Moon of Transformation,
My spirit sings of change,
For I have danced the rhythms
Of the thunder and the rain.
I have filled with laughter,
Ridding my heart of pain,
Embracing all the healing of
Emergence without blame.
I have bathed in sunlight,
I've ridden on the wind,
I have learned the lessons
Of becoming my best friend.
Mold my path with gladness,
As my vision comes into me,
Taking root in the present,
Becoming tangible reality.

The Clan Mother of the Thirteenth Moon Cycle, Becomes Her Vision,
teaches us that we are constantly becoming. We grow and change moment
by moment. The Blue Moon of Transformation signals that all human
beings have the right to grow and to change. If humans feel stagnation in
their paths, they may call upon Becomes Her Vision to assist them in
changing the stagnation into further growth, allowing their emergence to
begin again.

EMERGENCE
✂

The emergence of the butterfly from the cocoon is a miracle of the natural world. Every time a human being watches that miracle of transformation, there is a change in that human's perception of life, change, and rebirth.

The chrysalis is the looking-within place that nurtures any human being's sense of becoming. In order to *become our visions*, we must go to the deepest core of who and what we are—observing everything with wonder. Then the leap of faith that brings emergence does not contain fear, but is based in personal trust and knowing.

If it is time for you to take the leap of faith in some situation in your life, take heart. The emergence of your new potential is at hand. Going backward never works out. If you are afraid, list everything you can trust about yourself. It works!

THE RIGHT TO CHANGE
✂

All people have the right to change and to grow beyond their former limitations. In ancient times, when the misconduct of people in a Tribe was addressed by the Council of Elders, these people were given a chance to change their behavior. If they did not change their actions, they received a punishment that was determined by the Elders. Final punishments could result in banishment or death.

To break the harmony of a Tribe—to steal, to physically harm another, to lie, or to cheat—was not acceptable. Every person was given one chance to make amends to the other members of the Tribal family, showing his or her regret by making up the damage done. If the infraction happened again, the Elders were in charge of the punishment.

The right to change, and to be welcomed back into the Circle, is a *privilege* that allows a person to willingly repair the damage done. To understand and correct one's wrongdoing is the road to change. Any honest desire to change strengthens the individual spirit through admission of wrongdoing and through personal, humble amends.

ASKING FOR TRANSFORMATION
✖

Ferret was ready for his Rite of Passage. He had passed thirteen winters and had already been on one hunting party's journey as the moccasin boy. He was proud of the new responsibilities he had been given. During the journey, he had tended the ponies, kept all of the men's moccasins in good repair, and always had dry footwear available for each hunter.

Three moons had passed since then, and he was anxious for his next step in assuming the roles of a warrior. Approaching the Elder of his Clan, he stood silently and waited to be acknowledged, respecting his Elder's Sacred Space. It was a while before White Puma looked up. Seeing the youngster, he gave a hand signal showing permission to speak.

"Uncle, I would like to learn the next step of my Rite of Passage into manhood."

"I see that you waited a while, Ferret. Your next step has just been completed. You had the courage of a man, coming to me with respect and asking. Like your namesake, you ferreted out what the next step was supposed to be. One of the lessons any warrior learns is to have the courage to ask when something is not clear. It does not show that the man is stupid; it shows that the man is willing to discover, and to learn. Since you have chosen to be brave, it means that you also have the courage to face your night alone on the mountain. It is good."

Is it time for you to ask for the next step in your personal transformation? If so, the answers can be ferreted out through your courage and persistence.

MEDICINE BROTHER SONG
✂

Hear my words, oh Brother Warrior.
Let them ring bright and true.
The time is now, to be your vision,
For the world has need of you.

Ride the wind, oh peaceful warrior,
To the place that holds your pain.
Release the hurt that stops your vision,
Then open wide to love again.

We can dream with our Ancestors,
We can greet the Morning Star.
Together we can find the way,
To be proud of who we are,
To become the visions that we are.

So sail high, my Eagle Dancer,
Circle through the winds of change;
So walk free, my vision seeker,
Feel and heal and love again.

Then stand tall, my spirit warrior,
Glory in the light you seed.
Then dream on, my heart healer.
The love inside is all you need.
The love inside is all you need.

Reminder: *We all have the potential to become our visions—the love inside is all we need.*

USEFULNESS
✂

Native Americans honor the usefulness of everything in life. Everything has a purpose, a mission of service to the whole. It may not be apparent to some people, but the degree of its usefulness can determine an object's value.

Pencils and pens are highly valued in countries where they are scarce and where the people want their children to learn. Containers are valuable because with them it takes less time to transport more. Everything that has a use is serving humankind in some way, and many things have uses that are different from these objects' original purposes.

My Elders taught me that we should use what we have until it is worn out or until it can be used for another purpose. Food and supplies are to be shared with others you are hosting. If you run out, that is a sign of your family's generosity, giving all you have.

We need to understand that when we use our material things to serve a purpose, taking care of these things to increase their longevity, we will have honored the mission of that tool or object. This concept of the usefulness of the things that serve us is not unlike the human desire to feel useful, to find a place in life, and to have a sense of purpose. If we can find the relationship between having tools and being tools, having beautiful things and Walking in Beauty, and using our resources to increase their potentials, we can transform our lives, becoming *our* highest potentials.

BLUE MOON

Life is all about growing,
Of coming to many ends,
Only to find the door open,
And beginning once again.
On the trail of becoming,
Our visions light our way,
'Til dreaming and creating
Take form within the clay.
Molding every essence of
Our hopes, dreams, and fears,
Urging us ever onward through
The laughter and the tears.
The beauty of our humanness
May be a secret, and yet . . .
It is our deepest longing
To live without regret.
The fear of our failures
Can blind our inner sight,
But the Blue Moon of Becoming
Still shines . . .
    reflecting
        our vision's light.

SERENITY

The young woman looked at her Grandmother's face and saw a smile that reflected the sweetness of acceptance and grace. She knew that the Old One was nearly ready to Drop Her Robe. Grandmother spoke of her life to the young one, passing some wisdom to her granddaughter before she made ready to walk into the Spirit World.

"Two Feathers, you are young, and the words I have for you may not make sense to you for a while, but I must say them. I have earned every wrinkle on my face, and I find them beautiful. These wrinkles mark the paths I have followed and the lessons I have learned. These wrinkles remind me of the serenity in my heart. I have used the strength of my body to serve the People. I have used the curiosity of my mind to discover the truth. I have used the gifts of my spirit to connect to the Earth Mother and the Creator, and I have used the fire in my heart to love without judgment. The winter of my life has taught me many things. I am happy to have used all my gifts. I am content with my passage because I have given purpose to every part of my being. Now that all those things are used up, I am at peace. I have completed the vision that was given me. In time, you will find this state of grace and you will know that every step you take on the Path of Beauty honors the memory of those Ancestors who walked it before you, clearing the way."

EXPECTATIONS

Expectations show us
A mirror of our minds;
There lies the reflection
Of what we cannot find.
Bound to our limitations,
Blocked by doubts and fears,
The patterns of generations,
Their sorrows and their tears.
If we let go of those burdens,
And stand, in present time,
Trusting in Great Mystery,
To create the sublime.
A vision more complete,
Beyond our human sight,
Will appear on the horizon,
Born from grace and light.
Without the expectations,
We are free to see,
The workings of Creation
Within Great Mystery.
There lies our potential,
Within that state of grace,
The legacy of humankind,
Of every creed and race.

FEELING COMING CHANGE
✄

Sometimes there is a feeling that pervades our senses. We know that something *big* is about to happen. It can frighten us and make us desperately want to look around future's corner, just to get a glimpse of what we cannot see from our human vantage point.

Coming change is one of the mysteries of life that sets the wheels of emotion spinning. A tirade of feelings can blanket a person who is aware of his or her emotions, creating near panic. This type of panic comes with the human fear of the unknown. The two extremes are denial or numbness on one hand, with fearful expectation or projection on the other.

Transformation can be a wonderful process if we do not let our minds get in the way. There is a rhyme and reason for everything in Great Mystery's plan. How these events are played out, and how we humans respond to them, is dependent upon our personal viewpoints. When we embrace change as a part of growth, it can be exciting and joyful. We can then continue to feel the emotions and release our fears. When we become obsessed with second guessing, or reliving our past through our fears, we lose the magic. Our focus will determine how we weather every Rite of Passage in our lives. Crow teaches us the Divine Law of Creation; if we peck at the negative, it will come alive. If we peck at the positive, it will flourish. The choice is always ours; it never rests outside of our personal thoughts or Sacred Spaces.

What do you choose to feel pertaining to the coming changes in your life?

EMBRACING THE REALIZED SELF
✖

You are coming,
  I can feel your nearness;
    The wait has been so very long.

I have seen you in my dreams,
      knowing that you, too,
        were waiting for me.
Your silhouette,
    on the horizon of my mind,
        has made me anxious.
I am ready to share my cup with you,
    to drink the draught of our creation.
I can feel you in this room,
    smiling on my anxiousness . . .
With you has come the scent of mountain sage;
      you knew.
My preparation goes on,
    so that I can be the chalice of your beingness.
Please hurry,
  So swift a taste of your loving space
      has left my heart fluttering.
You have gone,
      but I reverently await your return.

CHANGING THE VISION
✶

Every person has the right to change the vision of who and what they choose to be. As we grow, what we want from life changes. When we see how we can contribute and grow, we often choose to change what we originally wanted from life at an earlier time. The change in direction, or in purpose, is one form of transformation. When we change any course of action, we may discover new paths that will allow us to respond to life in a different manner. Growing with, and into, these different directions can reveal parts of our evolving Selves that had never before been allowed self-expression.

Prior to our decisions to grow, transformation may have been something other people did. We may have seen life-threatening situations force changes on those who lived in fear of change. When we *choose* to change our visions of life, and of our potential, we are evolving from personal choice. Transformation brings our choices into clear view and gives us a gift. That gift of *completion* contains another corridor of potential experience that offers a world of new choices.

If you have come to a crossroad, give yourself a celebration for having come that far; then honor all of the new choices you have by taking off the blinders!

CELEBRATE YOURSELF!

✖

Show that you honor the sacredness of your spirit, the agility of your body, the support of your spine and bone structure, the way that your feet meet the ground, giving balance to your earthly form. Notice the sparkle in your eyes and the willingness of your body to move to the rhythms of your heartbeat. Honor your ability to think and reason. Stand tall and draw upon your human grace as you walk with the pleasure found in muscle and bone, moving in unison with the strength of your inner purpose!

This is how all living things express the grace of physicality, to the level of their own abilities. Celebrating physicality reflects to humankind the aliveness of spirit in motion. The creatures of the natural world teach us how to celebrate our human physicality. Through them, we learn to celebrate the body's ability to move, each person to the degree his or her body is able, learning harmony.

Becomes Her Vision, the Clan Mother of the Thirteenth Moon Cycle, reminds us that through movement and the body's expression, we are celebrating our humanness. The unity of body, heart, mind, spirit, and will creates a kind of harmony that gives birth to personal transformation. Without celebrating our ability to move the human body, the miracle of personal creation becomes stagnant. Is it time to rediscover the pleasure of physical agility and to move your body's energy? Go ahead; give yourself reason to celebrate your human physical potential! The whole process may astound you.

FINAL FRONTIER
✂

Humans tend to look for adventure when they are willing to celebrate their aliveness. Could it be that the final frontier facing humankind is the discovery of the integrated individual?

What is an integrated individual?

A person who knows and honors his or her uniqueness as it flows within the Oneness of Creation, living at peace within that harmony. The integrated individual retains his or her uniqueness by simply being.

The adventures awaiting the human spirit who approaches this final frontier to wholeness will be as varied as each explorer's imagination. How the adventure unfolds depends upon each traveler's willingness to grow, serving the whole. Discovering the mysteries of life and bearing witness to the unfoldment takes courage and faith. The final destination is always the same—transformation!

BECOMES HER VISION
⚒

The waking dream comes to life,
And lives her vision through me.
Emerging from the chrysalis,
She sets her healed heart free.

Mother of the seeds of change,
Who nurtures them as they grow,
You planted a dream in my heart
To illuminate all that I know.

You taught me how to give away
My fear of becoming the dream,
Showing me how to walk my truth,
Reclaiming self-love and esteem.

As I become all that I am,
Then together we shall fly,
The spirit of transformation
Reflected in Condor's eye.

Becomes Her Vision, the Clan Mother of the Thirteenth Moon Cycle, appears when we are ready to take the leap of faith and live the realized dream. She lovingly assists us over the humps that mark every change in our lives. She watches us while we grow, nurturing every step toward wholeness, reminding us that our transformation also entails being a guiding force for others. Reach out to some brother or sister who may be confused or feeling alone. Have you ever had someone bless your life in your darkest hour? Whether you answer yes or no, you know inside how much it did make, or could have made, a difference. To dare is how we show the Creator our willingness to be.

ONE TRANSFORMS TO ONENESS
✖

GREAT MYSTERY AND THE UNIVERSE
ARE ONE AND THE SAME THING: A
WHOLENESS—AGAINST WHICH ALL
SEPARATION BECOMES MEANINGLESS.

Becomes Her Vision, the Clan Mother of the Thirteenth Moon Cycle, shows us our potential transformation as she enlightens us as to the overview of the Great Mystery. If we understand that we are always on the path of becoming, we come to know that we are constantly evolving. There is no separation between the human spirit and the human potential. There is no separation between All Life and the Great Mystery. All separation is illusion, and these illusions are created inside the human mind.

VISIGNS

Before crossing over, the Holy Man called a Circle, a council meeting. The younger men who had looked to the Old One for guidance were anxious to hear his words. The Holy Man spoke of visions, of aspirations, and of dreams.

"In every person's life, they may have one vision of what they want to be. It may take every winter of that person's life to fully understand these glimpses of his or her path. Understanding the signs that guide you lies in seeing that the path is not outside of daily life. The road to attaining your victory is made of your faith. The challenges are made of personal weaknesses. The rocky trails are made of stubbornness, pride, and arrogance. The swamps are made from self-doubt, lack of courage, and mistrust. Those who seem to hinder your progress are showing you the places inside of yourself where you are split in two, taunting and criticizing your resolve to count coup.

"In my walk, I have seen many who blamed the Great Mystery for their failures. Many who raged against other outside forces, breaking faith with their families and friends. Many more who refused the gifts of compassion and forgiveness that could have given them strength, choosing instead the false pride of self-importance.

"The road to becoming your vision is always straightforward. Your potential and your role is always personal. That personal vision of yourself can be accessed and attained only when you have the courage to heal the enemy within."

BE WILD AND FOREVER FREE
✂

Blundering through the Mystery,
Seeking solace and change,
And the marriage of separation,
The wisdom of innocence retained.

Out of the darkness of the womb,
We clumsily grope for the light,
Submerging and then emerging,
Bearing witness to human plight.

Mastering the intellect,
  Dispelling the gloom,
    Sophistication comes to reign.
Out of order and chaos,
  We return to our dreams,
    The spirit and body reclaimed.

With primitive drives within us,
We must dance in order to be,
Blending lament and elation,
We become wild—and forever free.

FATE OR DESTINY?
⚓

HUMAN BOREDOM BREEDS LACK OF ATTENTION. IN
THE MOMENTS WHEN BOREDOM KEEPS PEOPLE FROM
BEING FULLY AWARE, THEY HAVE THE TENDENCY TO
DANGLE AT THE EDGE OF UNCONSCIOUSNESS. IT IS AT
THESE PRECARIOUS, INATTENTIVE TIMES THAT FATE
CAN SUPPLANT CHOSEN DESTINY.

Fate is the life path that is predetermined by our lack of attention
to our choices. Fate can slip up on the unaware because they are not
farsighted enough to see the results of their thoughts, actions, and
habit patterns. They do not use personal will.

Destiny is the open-ended patterns of possibilities and probabilities that are fashioned and directed through conscious choices
and freewill. All human beings have the same destiny: learning what
their gifts are and using those gifts to become their highest potential,
to become their visions.

How individuals use freewill and their uniqueness to fashion
the path of their destiny is as varied as each personal desire.
Attentiveness instead of boredom allows humans to become conscious of the way they are continually creating the destiny they
choose. If people are unconscious about having choices, they are
forced to accept the experiences that they allow others to dictate for
them. The result is a fate of other-determined expectations that
exclude having a personal vision, leaving dissatisfaction and a low
sense of personal worth in their wake. Fate or destiny, which do
you choose?

LOSS OF INTEGRITY
✂

The cultures and civilizations of our world that used people's word as their bond originally built dreams that served humanity. These brief golden moments in Earth's histories were continually supplanted when human beings acquired shallow, *marketplace souls.* When the greed set in, people allowed their basic spiritual and human values to be betrayed for money or power. The marketplace soul mentality persists in our present world.

Regaining one's personal values begins with ultimate honesty toward the Self. Integrity grows with each declined invitation to deny the truth. With growing ease, loyalty to the Self returns, allowing the impeccable spiritual warrior to emerge. That warrior part of the Self is fully armed with integrity, ready to embrace the vision held in her or his heart.

Is it time to reclaim some part of your integrity? Did you sell out some part of your personal dream by working in a job that you hate? Have you denied your warrior self's ability to reclaim the loyalty and integrity needed to become your vision? If we want to make a difference in this world, that change must begin inside of us.

PROWESS

⑋

The prowess of the visionary
Will continue to unfold,
As long as there are dreamers,
And new wonders to behold.

Brave hearts filled with boldness
Face the frontiers of the soul,
Banishing their hesitation as
They face the Unknown's goal.

Stretching the edge of reality,
Imagining what they can become,
Instead of being fragmented,
They march to freedom's drum.

Claiming their deepest passion,
The will's desire To be—
They take their places as warriors
By embracing infinity.

The prowess of the dreamer,
Is a wonder, filled with grace,
The legacy of Great Mystery
Given to every creed and race.

THIRST FOR WHOLENESS
✖

The young warrior traveled a long way to learn from the Holy Man, whose repute had brought honor to his Nation. The holes in the young brave's moccasins and the blisters on his feet attested to the ravages of his three-moon-long journey.

After having shared a Pipe and a meal, the young man spoke to the Holy Man, asking if the Wise One would accept him into his camp. The young traveler explained that he was willing to learn the Medicine Ways, to hunt for the Old One and his family, and to honor the Holy Man's Medicine.

The pregnant silence that followed was a long one, making the young man uncomfortable and fearful he would be rejected. The Wise One insisted that he be able to test the young brave before he gave his answer. It was agreed, and the following morning the test began.

The Holy Man had the brave look into the lake at his own image, then, with incredible strength, he shoved and held the young one's head underwater until he nearly drowned. After the ordeal, the young brave lay gasping for air. Finally able to speak, he asked his teacher, "Why?" The Holy Man asked the brave what he wanted most while he was below the water. The brave told him he wanted air, the breath of life.

The Holy Man nodded, and then said, "If you can thirst for wholeness in the way your body craved air while your head was under the water, you will have *earned* the right to learn the Sacred Teachings that I can share."

LIMITING THE UNIVERSE
✖

The majority of human beings see a limited universe because of their belief systems. When we have *not* been taught that perception can be manipulated and expanded—through the use of our imaginations—we lose the concepts that allow us to become our visions.

The universe of the Great Mystery is not The Absolute, it is The Ultimate Non-Absolute. We may expand our perceptions of life by embracing the idea that the essential, raw instability of the Great Mystery is constant, evolving Creation. By seeing ourselves as mirroring our individual, imagined parts of that creative growth process, we are able to flow harmoniously with the changes. Then it is easy to see why the universe will always remain an unfathomable mystery. How can we hold on to, and mentally limit, something that changes form in less time than it takes us to blink?

Through imagining what we wish to create, then merging with all stages of its manifestation, we become that vision. When we refuse to limit our imaginations, it becomes a little less astonishing when these imagined visions take form in tangible reality.

Can you see yourself in all of the stages of growth that it will take for you to become your vision? If you imagine it, you can make it happen! Remember to color yourself astonished when it works!

THE STATE OF GRACE
✂

Snow Tree was a talented healer and was studying the Medicine Ways with a Holy Man from his Clan. The final part of his training had to do with combining the talents of herbal cures, dreaming, counseling, diagnosis, Tribal Law and history, Medicine Stories, and Sacred Ceremonies. In order to serve the People, he would have to know which exact part of his training would best facilitate the proper results. The Holy Man watched without comment, as the people who needed assistance came one by one.

For one moon, Snow Tree worked alone for the People, while his teacher noted every decision, remedy, counseling session, and Doctoring Ceremony. At the end of that moon cycle, the Wise One commented. Snow Tree had done well, but he was still worried about one of his patients who had the wasting disease. The younger man had been well trained and he knew that he could only do his best, but his mind's nagging questions remained. The Holy Man saw his student's anguish and spoke to Snow Tree, giving him a final lesson through the Wise One's words.

"You have worked and learned with diligence, you have offered your gifts in integrity, and you have asked for spiritual guidance in all things. Now you must let go, surrendering yourself and your efforts to the *unseen* Healer. The Great Mystery offers you, and those who come for healing, the same gift. That gift can only be received if you let go. In giving over, not giving up, you will feel it. You may then come to know and to revere that gift; it is called the state of grace."

LOSING FACE
✂

The loss of credibility
Through actions of our own
Can bring a shame upon us,
Behavior we claim or disown.

The thunderous crash of ego,
Flashing with false integrity,
Tidal waves of self-importance
Are flooded with human debris.

This loss of face can haunt us,
Limiting our ability to transform,
Unless we work to lose the masks
That cause the ego's shameful storm.

Desire will hold the door open,
Humility welcomes us inside,
Change is always an option,
When we drop the masks of pride.

Losing the face of pretense
And owning a state of grace
Allows us to become our visions,
Being our truths, without disgrace.

TRANSFORMING INTO THE POTENTIAL

PERSONAL TRANSFORMATION CANNOT
BE GOVERNED BY RULES OR FORMAT,
ALLOWING OUR PERSONAL VISION TO
SURVIVE INTACT. FREEWILL IS HOW WE
REACH OUR ULTIMATE POTENTIAL.

Every person is unique. Transformation is always an individual process that uses the uniqueness of each human being and develops its own way of becoming. The timing is different for each person, the goals are varied, the vision is ultimately personal, and no part of *the process of becoming* is externally directed.

The personal will of human beings determines how they grow, how they change, what they sense, and what the outcome will be. To put rules or regulations on how a flower blooms would be ridiculous. No human, or human-made organization can force or subdue the process of internal change. Personal transformation is one of the mysteries of the life process that contains miraculous potentials.

If you are trying to become what others want you to be, these rules can keep your personal will in denial. If you are following a set lesson plan, it won't work. Is it time to let your heart's greatest joy take the lead? If so, you will find the ingredients that allow you to become your vision—in your own time and in your individual way.

BEING WILLING OR COMPELLED?

There are moments in life when people feel that they are being compelled to follow a certain course of action. The will is directing what they are doing, but there is an extra ingredient present that drives them to greater heights of experience.

Some call that extra force inspiration. In the root form of the word, inspiration means inhaling spirit, using and integrating that force to inspire. My Elders called that feeling "Walking with Spirit." Being inspired comes to all individuals when they allow the spirit of what they are doing to fill them with the sheer excitement of being. Inspiration is a transforming experience in and of itself.

If people have been doing a certain activity for years, without caring, and they suddenly become excited and inspired, the quality of what they are doing takes on a whole new perspective. When this occurs in a person's life, transformation is at hand. The individual is then directed by Spirit *and* will, creating a magical aliveness that animates every act of daily life. This is the beginning of the path that allows humans to become their visions.

EMERGING FROM THE CAVE OF BEAR

The Rite of Passage was underway as Becomes Her Vision directed the initiate in front of her to enter the Stillness, then, with the senses, to journey into the Cave of Bear, through the forehead, into the center of the skull.

The initiate traveled into the internal cave. It was dark, there were cobwebs, and no one had been here for a long time. The Clan Mother's voice told the initiate to get an imaginary torch and to follow the cave's tunnel to the end. There, the potential Self would be waiting. The Orenda, the Spiritual Essence, was awaiting discovery, longing for union.

The initiate was awed by the beauty of the vision and was directed to step inside the light of the Orenda, embracing the feelings. The wholeness of integration occurred as the two became one.

The Rite of Passage was complete when the initiate emerged from the Cave of Bear, returning to the tangible world with the Spiritual Essence and the vision of personal potential as a part of Self.

Becomes Her Vision smiled. Another human had emerged from the Cave of Bear, having seen the vision of what the Self was becoming. The guidance provided by the Rite of Passage created inner knowing. Every initiate who emerged from the Cave of Bear realized that the promise of personal potential was awaiting discovery, always available within the Self.

BLESSINGS OF THE BEAUTY WAY
✄

If there is tendency for a person to embrace the sheer pleasure of being human, it can be found through the Beauty Way. If our thoughts, actions, words, and manner of being are harmonious, we are Walking in Beauty.

To find the blessings of the Beauty Way, all we need to do is to make every act of life important and sacred. That may be a stretch for some people, but it is attainable. By making everything in our lives as sacred as possible, we learn to notice that the intricate steps of life's process are all blessings. Some steps may be challenging or may contain distressing feelings at the time, but there is always a hidden opportunity for growth.

Authentic freedom comes when we refuse to deny or to judge any part of our human process. We can learn to allow ourselves, and others, the personal feelings and individual points of view that comprise *the will.* We can learn to honor our dreams and aspirations, as well as honoring the unique goals of other individuals. We can learn to be accountable for our words and actions, holding personal worth and honesty in integrity's light. We can learn to reserve our energy for appropriate usage, nurturing the Self and others to the degree that it serves the wholeness of both. We can learn to heal the negative feelings of self-abuse and self-rejection, without denial, by choosing to feel these feelings without judging them. Through experiencing, expressing, and then moving these feelings, we can access freewill. We are then able to choose how we wish to change and heal our former negative thoughts. The freedom of feeling every emotion we have, without denial, allows us to access the sacred and empowering gifts of choice—freewill.

When we find the balance needed in our lives through trial and error, that process should not to be judged by counting the seeming failures along the way. The lessons of human growth are steps in developing our skills. All people have the ability to develop the skills necessary to attain the happiness they seek—if they are willing to learn from the challenges presented, without counting the mistakes as defeats. We could never achieve harmony without experiencing discord. Through the separation that is felt in discordant situations, we are then able to strive for harmony; if for no other reason, we choose harmony because it becomes pleasurable and desirable.

The Thirteen Original Clan Mothers are the aspects of the Earth Mother and Grandmother Moon Cycles that are available to guide us to the prosperous goal of Life, Unity, and Equality for Eternity. The lessons of the Beauty Way, and the ultimate value of the Clan Mother's creed, is a gift to us and to All Our Relations—that sacred legacy allows the world to become a vision of living Harmony.

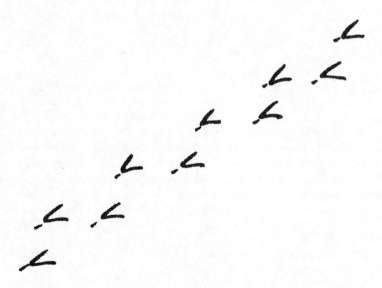

ABOUT THE AUTHOR

✂

Jamie Sams has captivated a wide audience with her knowledge, experience, pure-of-spirit presence, and natural ability to teach. She has created two best-selling guides to self-discovery through native traditions: *Sacred Path Cards™: The Discovery of Self Through Native Teachings* and, with David Carson, *Medicine Cards™: The Discovery of Power Through the Ways of Animals.* Her most recent book is *The Thirteen Original Clan Mothers.*